JIHAD IN MEDIAEVAL AND MODERN ISLAM

RELIGIOUS TEXTS TRANSLATION SERIES

NISABA

EDITED BY

M. S. H. G. HEERMA VAN VOSS, D. J. HOENS,
J. KNAPPERT, R. P. KRAMERS, B. A. VAN PROOSDIJ,
J. D. J. WAARDENBURG

VOLUME FIVE

dNisaba

E. J. BRILL — LEIDEN — 1977

JIHAD IN MEDIAEVAL AND MODERN ISLAM

THE CHAPTER ON JIHAD
FROM AVERROES' LEGAL HANDBOOK
'*BIDĀYAT AL-MUDJTAHID*'

AND

THE TREATISE '*KORAN AND FIGHTING*' BY
THE LATE SHAYKH AL-AZHAR, MAḤMŪD SHALTŪT

TRANSLATED AND ANNOTATED BY

RUDOLPH PETERS

E. J. BRILL — LEIDEN — 1977

NISABA is the name of the Sumerian goddess of vegetation and writing, whose symbol is the calamus (the instrument with which the writing was impressed on the soft clay) on an altar. The Sumerians were the first people to use writing, for keeping accounts and, by extension, inter alia, as a substitute for the oral tradition. For this reason, the goddess has been given pride of place here.

ISBN 90 04 04854 5

PRINTED IN BELGIUM

CONTENTS

ACKNOWLEDGEMENTS

First, I want to express my gratitude to Dr. J. D. J. Waardenburg for having encouraged me to publish these translations in the Nisaba-series. I am greatly indebted to Mrs. Dorinde van Oort who kindly assisted me in preparing the English text of the translations. Finally I want to thank Mrs. Alice Gastkemper for her painstaking care in typing the manuscript.

Amsterdam/Marrum (Fr.) RUDOLPH PETERS

I. INTRODUCTION

1. *Islamic Law*

The prescriptions concerning Holy War in Islam are part of the *Sharīʿah* or Islamic Law, which comprises far more than what we commonly understand by law. According to the current definition, *Sharīʿah* covers the whole of Allah's commands and prohibitions with regard to human behaviour. Side by side with e.g. matrimonial law, law of property, criminal law and law of succession, it includes for instance the prescriptions for religious worship (prayer, fasting, etc.).

In order to give the reader some idea about the relationship between the different sources of Islamic Law, I shall first give a survey of the traditional Islamic theory of the origin and development of the *Sharīʿah*. According to this theory, Allah's commands have been made known primarily in his revelation, the Koran, which, according to the Islamic doctrine, contains Allah's words. However, only a small number of the Koranic verses are in the form of explicit rules. Often extremely specific and detailed, they were obviously revealed with reference to concrete events. When it appeared after Mohammed's death (632 A.D.) that, in many cases, the Koran failed to provide a solution, the acts and pronouncements of the Prophet were resorted to as a second source. In the course of the third century of the Hijrah (ca. ninth century A.D.), these Traditions, which had originally been related orally, were recorded and codified in compilations. Neither of these sources, Koran and Tradition, are, however, very systematic; often they are even contradictory. At a later date, a set of rules came into being with regard to the hierarchy of sources etc., and by means of these rules it was attempted to systematize the material. When two prescriptions were obviously at variance and could not be reconciled, it was assumed that the one rule had abrogated the other one. However, the Traditions, along with the Koran, did not suffice either, for as a result of the problems caused by the great Islamic conquests and the rapid social changes, the lawyers were still confronted with many cases for which they could not find a solution. Consequently, they resorted to interpretation. They mostly made use of analogous interpretation, which was to the effect that to a case for which no solution had been given, the rules belonging to a resembling case were applied. It was assumed that underlying both cases was the same *ratio*. In order to lend authority to this human interpretation, the doctrine of the *Consensus* (*idjmāʿ*) was established. Tradition has it that the Prophet said: "*My congregation will never be agreed about an error*". From this it was inferred that when the Moslems (or the lawyers) were agreed on a rule, there could be no question of an error. *Consensus* (*idjmāʿ*) as well as analogous interpretation (*qiyās*) were given the status of source of law. In the course of the third century after the Hijrah (ninth century A.D.), the opinion took form that it was no longer possible, in view of the corruption of the times, to interpret the sources independently. Henceforth, the doctrines of the illustrious predecessors had to be followed. This is called *taqlīd* (to invest with authority, to follow blindly). Free interpretation of the sources (*idjtihād*) was no longer considered to be allowed. This was called the "*Closing of the gate of idjtihād*". Only recently, by the end of the 19th century and along with Islamic Modernism, a new tendency arose which claimed the right to *idjtihād*. In the meantime, modern research has proved that the Islamic conception as described above could not stand the test of historical criticism. According to the now current view, Islamic law was founded on the customary law of Medina and Mecca and on the administrative and fiscal practice of the first caliphs. In this early period, little attention was paid to the prescriptions of the Koran. It was not until later that the raw subject-material underwent a process of islamization, after the introduction of and comparison with the Koran prescriptions, and that the subject-material was systematized. Rules that could not be traced back to the Koran were cast into the form of Traditions dating back to the Prophet.

2. *The "Holy War"*

Only one kind of war has been sanctioned and regulated by Islamic law, viz. the jihad, known in Western literature as "Holy War". This is the war against unbelievers. Since Islamic law proceeds on the ideal of one Islamic state, such as it existed during the first hundred years after Mohammed's death, another kind of war would be inconceivable, warfare against Islamic rebels excepted. The primary aim of the jihad is not, as it was often supposed in the older European literature, the conversion by force of unbelievers, but the expansion — and also defence — of the Islamic state. Unbelievers who were brought under Islamic rule in this manner were given a choice. Either they were allowed, in return for the payment of a special tax, to abide by their own religion (cf. the translation, par 7), or they could become converts to Islam, in which case they acquired full civil rights.

It may well be questioned whether the term "Holy War" is an adequate translation of the concept jihad. By "Holy

War" is commonly understood a war which is conducted exclusively or almost exclusively for religious reasons. Islamic law, however, does not distinguish between state and religion. The Moslem's entire sphere of action, and also that of the head of state, is subject to Islamic law, which also provides prescriptions for warfare. Again, Islamic law proceeds on the ideal of one Islamic state. This means, *ipso facto*, that the remaining states are non-Islamic and consequently potential enemies.

That the jihad has been defined as warfare against the unbelievers does not necessarily mean, therefore, that such a war is founded exclusively on religious motives. Historically speaking, there has often rather been question of purely political grounds, such as the wish for expansion of territory or the necessity to defend it against attacks from outside. "Holy War" is thus, strictly speaking, a wrong translation of "jihad", and the reason why it is nevertheless used here is that the term has become current in Western literature.

The concept jihad, however, covers not only a collective aspect, the conducting of a war by the Islamic state, but also a personal one. The participation of a Moslem in such a war is also called jihad and is considered a pious act that stands on the same level as asceticism and other good works. Numerous are the Koran-verses and Traditions in which Paradise is promised to those who fall in battle. Therefore it is likely that many Moslems took part in a war on the ground of personal and religious motives. In this sense it might be called a "Holy War", but in the past as well as recently these religious sentiments have been exploited by rulers with a view to mobilize the people for wars. In fact, this is the reason why the Arab-Israeli wars have occasionally been called jihad. This might be compared to the blessing of arms by clergy, customary in the Western world : the war is given religious sanction and there is no need for the believer to ask further questions.

In the classical codes of law, the chapters on jihad cover a wide range of rules. They codify, as far as possible, all the rights and obligations of the individual Moslem (including those of the Imam, the head of the Islamic state) in his relation to unbelievers who have not been subjected to Islamic rule. As to the legitimacy of warfare against these, i.e. the conditions which will justify war against them (*jus ad bellum*), they are not over-explicit. Modern treatises are different in this respect : in order to counter the rather distorted view of the jihad that is commonly held in the West, modern Moslems especially emphasize the following aspect : claiming the right to *idjtihād*, the new interpretation of the sources, they profess that the jihad is essentially defensive warfare, striving to protect the Islam and the Moslems and to guarantee the propagation of the Islamic mission.

3. *Averroes*

Averroes (Ar. : Abū al-Walīd Muḥammad Ibn Muḥammad Ibn Rushd) was born of a family of lawyers, in the then Arabic town of Córdoba, in 1126 A.D. His grandfather and namesake had written a number of works on Islamic law which enjoyed great popularity and it was as a matter of course that Averroes followed in the footsteps of his ancestors. He held the post of judge (*qāḍī*) in Sevilla and in his native town Córdoba, but he also became known as a physician — he was the court-physician of the Almohad prince Abū Yaʿqūb (who reigned from 1162 until 1184) — and as a philosopher. It is in this latter quality that he achieved fame in Europe, especially through his comments on the works of Aristotle. In the Islamic world, on the other hand, he remained famous chiefly as a lawyer. He died in Marrakesh (Morocco) in 1198.

His best known legal handbook is *Bidāyat al-Mudjtahid wa-Nihāyat al-Muqtaṣid* (lit.: The beginning for him who interprets the sources independently and the end for him who wishes to limit himself). With the exception of the chapter on pilgrimage (*ḥadjdj*), which he did not finish until 1188, he wrote the work around the year 1167, when he accepted the post of *qāḍī*. The book belongs to the genre of *ikhtilāf*-works. These are treatises in which the opinions of the different schools are juxtaposed and in which the controversies (*ikhtilāf*) between the early lawyers are discussed. Although traditional as far as contents are concerned, the manner of presentation of the *Bidāyah* is original. In his treatment of each controversy, Averrroes enters deeply into the different arguments underlying it. Usually, he reduces the controversy to a disagreement about the question of how two conflicting Koran-verses or Traditions are related to each other. This often boils down to the question whether the one rule is a general one and the other an exception, or whether the one rule has abrogated the other. However ingenious these reasonings may be, it is to be kept well in mind that this is a matter of *hineininterpretieren*. The prescriptions of Islamic Law had already been formulated soon after Mohammed's death, the theoretical foundations with Koran-verses and Traditions followed later. Averroes was an adherent of the Malikite School, the ruling one in Islamic Spain. Nevertheless he juxtaposes the opinions of the different Schools with impartiality and refrains from passing judgements on the validity of the arguments brought forward. The only indication that he is a Malikite might be found in the fact that he sometimes expatiates a little longer on the controversies within this school.

Literature about the juridical activities of Averroes:
R. Brunschvig, *Averroës juriste*, in: *Études d'Orientalisme, dédiées à la mémoire de Lévi-Provençal*. Paris, Maisonneuve, 1962, part I, pp. 35-68.
L. Bercher, *Averroës "Bidayat al-Mujtahid"*, *Revue Tunisienne de Droit*, 1955, no. 3/4, pp. 30-37 (translation of the introduction to the *Bidāyah*, in which Averroes expounds his method).

4. *Maḥmūd Shaltūt*

Maḥmūd Shaltūt was born on April 23, 1893, in the small provincial town of Minyah Banī Manṣūr in Lower Egypt. After his traditional Islamic education in Alexandria, he became a teacher at the Azhar University in Cairo, the oldest and most famous institution for religious studies in the Islamic world. He was fired in 1931 for being an advocate of reform of the Azhar. When the climate had changed and certain reforms had been introduced, he was allowed to return and was nominated Dean of the *Sharī'ah*-faculty. Henceforth he occupied several important posts at the University, until he was appointed *Shaykh al-Azhar* by presidential decree in 1958. He died on December 12, 1963.

Shaltūt was a prolific author on Islamic topics and especially on the legal aspects of Islam. He belonged to the modernist school of Muḥammad 'Abduh and Muḥammad Rashīd Riḍa, whose influences are clearly discernible in all his writings. His first publication on jihad dates from 1933, when two of his lectures were published in book-form under the title: "*The Mohammedan Mission and Fighting in Islam*" (*al-daʿwah al-muḥammadiyyah wa-al-qitāl fī al-Islām*, Cairo: al-Maṭbaʿah al-Salafiyyah, 1352 H., 41 pp.). Parts of it were included in his book "*The Koran and Fighting*" (*al-Qur'ān wa-al-qitāl*), which he wrote in 1940. It was published in 1948.

5. *Editions*

For the translation of the "*Bidāyah*" I used two nearly identical Cairo editions. The points wherein they differ are of minor importance and mainly due to printing errors. The first one was printed in 1960 at Muṣṭafā al-Bābī al-Ḥalabī's; the second by Dār al-Fikr/Maktabat Khāngī (no date). For the translation of "*The Koran and Fighting*" I used the 1948 edition (published by Maṭbaʿat al-Naṣr/Maktab Ittiḥād al-Sharq) as well as the 1951 one (ed. by Dār al-Kitāb al-ʿArabī). For the quotations from the Koran I made use of Bell's translation (Edinburgh, 1939).

THE CHAPTER ON JIHAD FROM AVERROES' LEGAL HANDBOOK AL-BIDĀYAH

b~ 1126 AD.

The jihad

The most important rules concerning this subject will be dealt with in two chapters. The first will contain the most important regulations as regards warfare, the second the rules pertaining to the enemy's property when it is captured by the Moslems.[1]

The first chapter consists of seven paragraphs :

1. The legal qualification (*ḥukm*) of this activity and the persons who are obliged to take part in it.
2. The enemy.
3. The damage allowed to be inflicted upon the different categories of enemies.
4. The prerequisites for warfare.
5. The maximum number of enemies against which one is obliged to stand one's ground.
6. Truce.
7. The aims of warfare.

Par. 1. The legal qualification (*ḥukm*) of this activity and the persons obliged to take part in it.

Scholars agree that the jihad is a collective not a personal obligation. Only ʿAbd Allāh Ibn al-Ḥasan [2] professed it to be a recommendable act. According to the majority of scholars, the compulsory nature of the jihad is founded on [K 2:216] : "*Fighting is prescribed for you, though it is distasteful to you*".[3] That this obligation is a collective and not a personal one, i.e. that the obligation, when it can be properly carried out by a limited number of individuals, is cancelled for the remaining Moslems, is founded on [K 9:112] : "*It is not for the believers to march out all together*",[4] on [K 4:95] : "*Though to all, Allah hath promised the good* (*reward*)" [5] and, lastly, on the fact that the Prophet never went to battle without leaving some people behind. All this together implies that this activity is a collective obligation. The obligation to participate in the jihad applies to adult free men who have the means at their disposal to go to war and who are healthy, that is, not ill or suffering from chronic diseases. There is absolutely no controversy about the latter restriction because of [K 48:17] : "*There is no blame upon the blind, or upon the lame, or upon the sick*" [6] and because of [K 9:91] : "*No blame rests upon the frail or upon the sick or upon those who find nothing to contribute*".[7] Nor do I know of any dissentient views as regards the rule that this obligation applies only to free men. Nearly all scholars agree that this obligation is conditional on permission granted by the parents. Only in the case that the obligation has become a personal one, for instance because there is nobody else to carry it out, can this permission be dispensed with.[8] This prerequisite of permission is based on the following authentic Tradition : "*Once a man said to the Messenger of Allah* : '*I wish to take part in the jihad*'. *The Messenger said to him* : '*Are both your parents still alive?*' *When he answered in the affirmative, the Messenger said* : '*Then perform the jihad for their sake*' ". Scholars are not agreed whether this permission is also required of parents who are polytheists. There is controversy, too, about the question whether the creditor's permission has to be asked when a person has run into debt. An argument in favour of this can be found in the following Tradition : "*A man said to the Prophet* : '*Will*

Allah forgive me my sins if I shall sacrifice myself patiently and shall be killed in the way of Allah (i.e. by taking part in the jihad)?' The Prophet said: 'Yes, with the exception of your debts. This Djibrīl has told me before'".[9] The majority of scholars do not consider it obligatory, especially not when the debtor leaves enough behind to serve as payment for his debts.

Par. 2. The Enemy.

Scholars agree that all polytheists should be fought. This is founded on [K 8:39]: "*Fight them until there is no persecution and the religion is entirely Allah's*".[10] However, it has been related by Mālik[11] that it would not be allowed to attack the Ethiopians and the Turks on the strength of the Tradition of the Prophet: "*Leave the Ethiopians in peace as long as they leave you in peace*". Questioned as to the authenticity of this Tradition, Mālik did not acknowledge it, but said: "People still avoid attacking them".

Par. 3. The damage allowed to be inflicted upon the different categories of enemies.

Damage inflicted upon the enemy may consist in damage to his property, injury to his person or violation of his personal liberty, i.e. that he is made a slave and is appropriated. This may be done, according to the *Consensus* (*idjmāʿ*) to all polytheists: men, women, young and old, important and unimportant. Only with regard to monks do opinions vary; for some take it that they must be left in peace and that they must not be captured, but allowed to go unscathed and that they may not be enslaved. In support of their opinion they bring forward the words of the Prophet: "*Leave them in peace and also that to which they have dedicated themselves*",[12] as well as the practice of Abū Bakr.[13]

Most scholars are agreed that, in his dealings with captives, various policies are open to the Imam [head of the Islamic state, caliph]. He may pardon them, enslave them, kill them, or release them either on ransom or as *dhimmī* [non-Moslem subject of the Islamic state], in which latter case the released captive is obliged to pay poll-tax (*djizyah*). Some scholars, however, have taught that captives may never be slain. According to al-Ḥasan Ibn Muhammad al-Tamīmī,[14] this was even the *Consensus* (*idjmā*ʿ) of the *Ṣaḥābah* [contemporaries of Mohammed that have known him]. This controversy has arisen because, firstly, the Koran-verses contradict each other in this respect; secondly, practice [of the Prophet and the first caliphs] was inconsistent; and lastly, the obvious interpretation of the Koran is at variance with the Prophet's deeds. The obvious interpretation of [K 47:4]: "*So when ye meet those who have disbelieved* (*let there be*) *slaughter until when ye have made havoc of them*" [15] is that the Imam is only entitled to pardon captives or to release them on ransom. On the other hand, [K 8:67]: "*It was not for a prophet to have prisoners so as to cause havoc in the land*",[16] as well as the occasion when this verse was revealed [viz. the captives of Badr] would go to prove that it is better to slay captives than to enslave them. The Prophet himself would in some cases slay captives outside the field of battle, while he would pardon them in others. Women he used to enslave. Abū ʿUbayd [17] has related that the Prophet never enslaved male Arabs. After him, the *Ṣaḥābah* reached unanimity about the rule that the People of the Book (*ahl al-kitāb*), both male and female, might be enslaved. Those who are of the opinion that the verse which prohibits slaying [K 47:4] abrogates the

Prophet's example, maintain that captives may not be slain. Others profess, however, that this verse does not concern itself with the slaughter of captives and that it was by no means intended to restrict the number of policies possible with regard to captives. On the contrary, they say, the fact that the Prophet used to slay captives adds a supplementing rule to the verse in question [K 47:4] and thus removes the occasion for the complaint that he omitted to kill the captives of Badr. These, now, do profess that the killing of captives is allowed.

It is only allowed to slay the enemy on the condition that *amān* [safe-conduct] has not been granted. There is no dissension about this among the Moslems. There is controversy, however, concerning the question who is entitled to grant *amān*. Everyone is agreed that the Imam is entitled to this. The majority of scholars are of the opinion that free Moslem males are also entitled to grant it, but Ibn Mādjishūn [18] maintains that in this case, it is subject to authorization by the Imam. Similarly, there is controversy concerning the *amān* granted by women and slaves. Ibn Mādjishūn and Saḥnūn [19] hold that *amān* granted by a woman is also subject to authorization by the Imam. Abū Ḥanīfah [20] has taught that the *amān* granted by a slave is only valid when the slave is allowed to join in the fighting.[21] The source of the controversy is that a general rule is in conflict with the analogous interpretation of another rule. The general rule is founded on the words of the Prophet: "*The blood(money) of all Moslems is equal. Even the humblest strives for their protection. Together, they make up a unity against the others*". These words, in their universality, imply that *amān* granted by a slave is valid. The conflicting analogy is that in order to be able to grant *amān*, full legal capacity is required. Now, a slave has only partial legal capacity by the very fact of his being a slave. By analogy, the fact that he is a slave should counteract the validity of his *amān*, as it does with regard to numerous other legal acts. The general rule, then, should be restricted by analogy.

The controversy about the validity of *amān* granted by a woman owes its origin to two different readings of the words of the Prophet: "*We grant protection to those to whom you have granted protection, Umm Hāni'*" as well as to the question whether women are to be put on a par with men by analogy. Some read in the words of the Prophet an authorization of the *amān* granted by Umm Hāni', not a confirmation of its validity, and they infer that her *amān* would have had no legal effects had the Prophet not authorized it. Consequently, they maintain that *amān* granted by a woman is only valid when the Imam has authorized it. Others hold that the Prophet confirmed the *amān* granted by Umm Hāni' in the sense that he approved something which already existed and had legal effects, not in the sense that the act was only validated by his authorization. Thus, the latter group maintains that a woman is entitled to grant valid *amān*. This view finds also favour with those who, in this respect, put women on a par with men and feel that there is no difference between them here. Others, who are of the opinion that a woman is inferior to a man, consider an *amān* granted by her invalid. Anyhow, *amān* does not afford protection against enslavement but only against death.[22] The controversy [about the validity of *amān* granted by women] might also be explained by the divergent opinions about the use of the male plural: does this include women or not? All this, of course, according to legal usage.

As regards injury to the person, that is, the slaying of the enemy, the Moslems agree that in times of war, all adult, able-bodied, unbelieving males may be slain. As to the question whether the enemy may also be slain after he has been captured, there is the above-mentioned controversy. There is no disagreement about the rule that it is forbidden to slay women and children, provided that they are not fighting, for then women, in any case, may be slain. This rule is founded on the fact that, according to authoritative Traditions, the Prophet prohibited the slaughter of women and children and once said about a woman who had been slain : "*She was not one who would have fought*".[23]

There is controversy about the question whether it is allowed to slay hermits who have retired from the world, the blind, the chronically ill and the insane, those who are old and unable to fight any longer, peasants, and serfs. Mālik professes that neither the blind, nor the insane, nor hermits may be slain and that of their property not all may be carried off, but that enough should be left for them to be able to survive. Neither is it allowed, according to him, to slay the old and decrepit. Of the same opinion are Abū Ḥanīfah and his pupils. Thawrī [24] and Awzāʿī,[25] however, have taught that of these groups, only the aged may not be slain. On the other hand, Awzāʿī had also taught that this prohibition is also valid with regard to peasants. According to the most authoritative opinion of Shāfiʿī,[26] all of these categories may be slain. The source of this controversy is to be found in the fact that in a number of Traditions, rules are given which are at variance with the general rule from the Book [i.e. the Koran] as well as with the general rule of the authentic Tradition : "*I have been commanded to fight the people until they say : 'There is no God but Allah'* ".[27] [K 9:5] : "*Then when the sacred months have slipped away, slay the polytheists wherever ye find them*"[28] as well as the above-mentioned Tradition give as a general rule that every polytheist must be slain, whether he is a monk or not. Nevertheless, the following Traditions, among others, are brought forward in support of the prescription that the lives of the categories mentioned must be saved: 1. Dāwūd Ibn al-Haṣīn[29] has related on the authority of ʿIkrimah[30] on the authority of Ibn ʿAbbās[31] that the Prophet used to say, whenever he sent out his armies: "*Do not slay hermits*". 2. On the authority of Anas Ibn Mālik[32] it has been related that the Prophet said: "*Do not slay the old and decrepit, children, or women. Do not purloin what belongs to the spoils*". Abū Dāwūd[33] included this Tradition in his compilation. 3. Mālik has related that Abū Bakr said: "*You will find people who will profess that they have dedicated themselves entirely to God. Leave them in peace and also that to which they have dedicated themselves*". 4. "*Do not slay women, nor infants, nor those worn with age*". However, it seems to me that the chief source for the controversy about this question is that [K 2:190]: "*Fight in the way of Allah those who fight you, but do not provoke hostility; verily Allah loveth not those who provoke hostility*" is in conflict with [K 9:5]: "*Then when the sacred months have slipped away, slay the polytheists wherever ye find them*".[34] Some maintain that K 9:5 has abrogated K 2:190, because at the outset it was only allowed to slay people who were able-bodied.[35] Consequently, the latter take it that K 9:5 gives a rule without exceptions. Others are of the opinion that K 2:190 has not been abrogated and that it is valid with regard to all those categories which do not take part in the fighting. According to these, K 2:190 gives an exceptive regulation as regards K 9:5. Shāfiʿī, in support of his interpretation, argues that it has been related on the authority of Sumrah [36] that the Prophet commanded: "*Slay the polytheists but spare their children*". The only motive why the enemy should be put to death, according to him, is their unbelief. This motive, then, goes for all unbelievers. Those who maintain that peasants are not to be slain argue that Zayd Ibn Wahb [37] has related: "*We received a letter from 'Umar,*[38] *saying: Do not purloin what belongs to the spoils, do not act perfidiously, do not slay babies and be god-fearing with regard to peasants*".[39] The prohibition to slay polytheist serfs is based on the Tradition of Rabāḥ Ibn Rabī'ah: "*Once, when Rabāḥ Ibn Rabī'ah sallied forth with the Messenger of Allah, he and (the) companions of the Prophet passed by a woman who had been slain. The Messenger halted and said: 'She was not one who would have fought.' Thereupon he looked at the men and said to one of them: 'Run after Khālid Ibn al-Walīd (and tell him) that he must not slay children, serfs or women'*". Basically, however, the source of their controversy is to be found in their divergent views concerning the motive why the enemy may be slain. Those who think that this is because they are unbelieving do not make exceptions for any polytheist. Others, who are of the opinion that this motive consists in their capacity for fighting, in view of the prohibition to slay female unbelievers, do make an exception for those who are unable to fight or who are not as a rule inclined to fight, such as peasants and serfs. Enemies must not be tortured nor must their bodies be mutilated. The Moslems agree that they may be slain with weapons. Controversy exists, however, concerning the question whether it is allowed to burn them by fire. Some consider it reprehensible to burn or to assail them with fire. This is also the opinion of 'Umar. It has been related that Mālik held a similar view. Sufyān al-Thawrī, on the other hand, considered it admissible. Others allow it only in case the enemy has started it. The source of this controversy is again in the fact that a general rule and a particular rule are at variance. The general rule is given by [K 9:5] : "*Slay the polytheists wherever ye find them*".[40] This does not preclude any manner of slaying. The particular rule is founded on an authoritative Tradition, according to which the Prophet said to a certain man : "*If ye should seize him, then slay him, yet do not burn him. No one is free to punish by means of fire, save the Lord of the (Hell) fire (i.e. Allah)*". Most scholars agree that fortresses may be assailed with mangonels, no matter whether there are women and children within them or not. This is based on the fact that the Prophet used mangonels against the population of al-Ṭā'if. Some, among whom is Awzāʿī, have taught that mangonels should not be resorted to when Moslem captives or children are within the [walls of the] fortress. Layth,[41] on the other hand, considered it admissible. The argument of those who do not allow it, reads [K 48:25] : "*Had they been separated out, We should have inflicted upon those of them who have disbelieved a punishment painful*".[42] Those who do allow it do so, as it were, with a view to the general interest. So much for the extent to which injury may be inflicted upon the person of the enemy.

Opinions vary as to the damage that may be inflicted on their property, such as buildings, cattle and crops. Mālik allowed the felling of trees, the picking of fruits and the demolishing of buildings, but not the slaughter of cattle and the burning of date-palms. Awzāʿī disapproved of the felling of fruit-trees and the demolishing of buildings, regardless of whether the buildings in question were churches or not. According to Shāfiʿī, dwellings and trees may be burnt as long as the enemy have the disposal of fortresses. When that is not the case, he considers it reprehensible to demolish buildings and to fell trees. The reason why there is this divergence of opinions is that the practice of Abū Bakr was at variance with that of the Prophet. According to an authoritative Tradition, the Prophet set fire to the palm-trees of Banū Naḍīr. On the other hand, it has been related as an irrefutable fact that Abū Bakr said : "*Do not fell trees and do not demolish buildings*". Some are of the opinion that Abū Bakr could only have spoken thus because he knew the practice of the Prophet to have been abrogated, since he would of course not have been at liberty to act in defiance of this practice had he known it. There are also those who take it that this policy of the prophet [did not give a general rule but] had reference only to Banū Naḍīr, since it was them who attacked him. Those who bring forward all these arguments adhere to the view of Abū Bakr. Others, however, go entirely by the practice of the Prophet. They maintain that it is impossible that anybody's words or deeds could be put forward as an argument against his practice and they consider it lawful to burn trees. Mālik makes a distinction between cattle and trees. According to him, the slaughter of cattle is torture, which is prohibited. Moreover, the Prophet is not related ever to have slain animals. So much for the extent to which it is allowed to inflict damage to the lives and property of the unbelievers.

Par. 4. The prerequisites for warfare.

According to all scholars, the prerequisite for warfare is that the enemy must have heard the summons to Islam. This implies that it is not allowed to attack them before the summons has reached them. All Moslems are agreed about this because of [K 17:15] : "*We have not been accustomed to punish until We have sent a messenger*".[43] However, there is controversy about the question whether the summons should be repeated when the war is resumed. Some hold that this is obligatory, others consider it merely recommendable, while according to a third group it is neither obligatory nor recommendable [and therefore a matter of indifference]. The source of this controversy is that the words and the deeds of the Prophet are at variance. According to an authoritative Tradition, the Prophet, when he sent out his armies, used to say to the leader: "*When ye will encounter your polytheist foes, then summon them to three things. Accept that which they consent to and refrain from* [*attacking*] *them. Summon them to conversion to Islam. If they consent to that, accept it and refrain from* [*attacking*] *them. Summon them thereupon to sally forth from their territory to the Abode of the Emigrants* (*muhādjirūn*) [*i.e. Medina*] *and impart to them that, if they do so, they will have the same rights and duties as the Emigrants. If they are unwilling to do so, however, and prefer to remain in their own territory, impart to them thereupon that they will be like the converted Beduins, who are subject to the same supreme authority of Allah as the* [*other*] *believers, but who are not entitled to a share in the spoils, unless they join the Moslems in the war. If they refuse that, then summon them to the payment of poll-tax. If they consent to that, accept it and refrain from* [*attacking*] *them. But if they refuse it, then invoke the help of Allah and attack them*". Nevertheless it has been related irrefutably that the Prophet repeatedly made sudden attacks upon the enemy at night or at dawn. Some, consequently, maintain, and they are in the majority, that the practice of the Prophet has abrogated his words. According to the latter, the relevant dictum dates back from an early period of Islam, before the summons had been propagated, because it contains a summons to emigration (*hidjrah*).[44] Others are of the opinion that more weight should be attached to the Prophet's words than to his deeds, because the latter are to be interpreted in the light of the particular circumstances. Those, lastly, who consider it recommendable, do so in order to reconcile both views.[45]

Par. 5. The maximum number of enemies against which one is obliged to stand one's ground.

The maximum number of enemies against which one is obliged to stand one's ground is twice the number [of one's own troops]. About this, everybody agrees on account of [K 8:66]: "*Now Allah hath made it lighter for you and knoweth that there is weakness among you*".[46] Ibn Mādjishūn maintains, on the authority of Mālik, that the actual force, rather than the number, is to be considered and that it might be allowed for a single man to flee before another if the latter should possess a superior horse, superior weapons and superior physical strength.

Par. 6. Truce.

The conclusion of truce is considered by some to be permitted from the very outset and without an immediate occasion, provided that the Imam deems it in the interest of the Moslems. Others maintain that it is only allowed when the Moslems are pressed by sheer necessity, such as a civil war and the like. As a condition for truce, it may be stipulated that the enemy pay a certain amount of money to the Moslems. This is not poll-tax (*djizyah*), because for that it would be required that they come under Islamic rule [which is not the case here]. Such a stipulation [the payment of a tribute], however, is not obligatory. Awzāʿī even considered it admissible that the Imam should conclude a truce with the stipulation that the Moslems pay a certain amount to the enemy, should this be forced upon them by emergency, such as a civil war and the like. Shāfiʿī's opinion is that the Moslems may never give anything to the unbelievers, unless they are in mortal fear of being extinguished, on account of the enemy's superiority or because they are being harrassed by disasters. Among those who profess that the Imam is entitled to conclude a truce when he considers it in the interest [of the Moslems] are Mālik, Shāfiʿī and Abū Ḥanīfah. Shāfiʿī maintains that a truce may not be concluded for a period longer than that of the truce which the Prophet concluded with the unbelievers in the year of Ḥudaybiyyah.[47] The controversy about the question whether the conclusion of truce is also allowed without a compulsive reason, is rooted in the fact that the obvious interpretation of [K 9:5] : "*Slay the polytheists wherever ye find them*" [48] and that of [K 9:29] : "*Fight against those who do not believe in Allah nor in the last day*",[49] contradict that of [K 8:61] : "*If they incline to make peace, incline thou to it, and set thy trust upon Allah*".[50] Some hold that the verse which commands the Moslems to fight the polytheists until they have been converted or until they pay poll-tax (*djizyah*) [K 9:29] abrogates the Peace-verse [K 8:61]. Consequently, they maintain that truce is only admissible in cases of necessity. Others are of the opinion that the Peace-verse [K 8:61] supplements the other two verses and they consider the concluding of truce allowed if the Imam deems it right. They also argue, in support of their view, that the Prophet acted accordingly, as the truce of Ḥudaybiyyah had not been concluded from necessity. According to Shāfi'ī, the principle is that polytheists must be fought until they have been converted or until they are willing to pay poll-tax (*djizyah*). The acts of the Prophet in the year of Ḥudaybiyyah are an exception to this [principle]. Therefore, says Shāfi'ī, a truce may never exceed the period for which the Prophet concluded truce in the case of Ḥudaybiyyah. Still, there is controversy about the duration of this period. According to some it amounts to four years, but according to others three or ten years. Shāfi'ī opts for the latter. As to the view of some, that in cases of emergency such as civil war and the like, the Moslems may conclude a truce on the stipulation that they pay the enemy a certain amount of money, this is based on the Prophet's example, for it has been related that he was seriously contemplating to bestow a third of the date-harvest of Medina upon a group of polytheists belonging to the Confederates with a view to induce them to move off. However, before he had had time to reach an agreement on the basis of the quantity of dates he had been allowed [by the people of Medina] to give away, Allah granted him the victory.[51] The opinion of those who profess that a truce may only be concluded when the Moslems are in mortal fear of extinction, is founded on analogous application of the rule that Moslem captives may be ransomed; for when Moslems have been reduced to such a state they are in the position of captives.

Par. 7. The aims of warfare.

The Moslems are agreed that the aim of warfare against the People of the Book, with the exception of those belonging to the Quraysh-tribe and Arab Christians, is twofold: either conversion to Islam, or payment of poll-tax (*djizyah*). This is based on [K 9:29]: "*Fight against those who do not believe in Allah nor in the last Day, and do not make forbidden what Allah and His messenger have made forbidden, and do not practice the religion of truth, of those who have been given the Book, until they pay the jizya off-hand, being subdued*". Most lawyers likewise agree that poll-tax (*djizyah*) may also be collected from Zoroastrians (*madjūs*) on the strength of the words of the Prophet: "*Treat them like the People of the Book*". There is, however, controversy with regard to polytheists who are not People of the Book: is it allowed to accept poll-tax (*djizyah*) from them or not? Some, like Mālik, have taught that it may be collected from any polytheist. Others make an exception for the polytheist Arabs. Shāfi'ī, Abū Thawr [52] and a few others maintain that poll-tax (*djizyah*) may only be accepted from People of the Book and Zoroastrians. The controversy is again brought about by the fact that a general rule conflicts with a particular one. The general rule is derived from [K 2:193 and 8:39]: "*Fight them until there is no persecution* (*i.e. persecution of believers by polytheists*), *and religion becomes Allah's*",[53] and from the Tradition: "*I have been commanded to fight the people until they say: 'There is no god but Allah'. When they say that, then their lives and property are inviolable to me, except* [*in the case when*] *the* [*law of*] *Islam allows it* [*to take them*]. *They will be answerable to Allah*". The particular rule is founded on the Tradition mentioned earlier,[54] viz. that Mohammed used to say to the leaders of troops which he sent out to the polytheist Arabs: "*When ye will encounter your polytheist foes, then summon them to three things*", etc. In this Tradition, poll-tax (*djizyah*) is also mentioned. Now, some scholars hold that a general rule cancels a particular one if the general rule was revealed at a later date. These do not accept poll-tax (*djizyah*) from others than People of the Book, since the verses prescribing, in general terms, to fight them are of a more recent date than the Tradition mentioned; for the general command to fight the polytheists is to be found in the *Sūrat Barā'ah*[55] which was revealed in the year of the conquest of Mecca.[56] The Tradition in question, on the other hand, dates back from before the conquest of Mecca, in view of the fact that it contains a summons to emigration.[57] Others, however, maintain that general rules should always be interpreted in association with the particular rules, no matter whether the one is more recent than the other or whether this is unknown. The latter group, accordingly, accepts poll-tax (*djizyah*) from any polytheist. The People of the Book are in an exceptional position with respect to the other polytheists because they have been excluded from the general rule just mentioned, on the strength of the particular rule given in [K 9:29]: "*... of those who have been given the Book, until they pay the jizya off-hand, being subdued*".[58] The poll-tax (*djizyah*) itself and the rules related to it will be dealt with in the next chapter. So much for the principles of warfare. One famous question remains to be touched upon in this connection: that whether it is prohibited to march into hostile territory carrying a copy of the Koran. Most scholars do not consider it allowed because an authoritative rule to this effect has been handed down from the Prophet in an authentic Tradition. Abū Ḥanīfah, on the other hand, has taught that it is allowed, provided that it is done under the protection of a strong and safe army. The source of this controversy is the question: was this prohibition put in general terms in order that it might hold good universally and without exceptions, or was the prohibition put in general terms while it was nevertheless intended as a particular rule?

THE KORAN AND FIGHTING

by

MAḤMŪD SHALTŪT 1893-1963 A.D.

1. THE EXEMPLARY METHOD OF KORAN INTERPRETATION

(*Summary*)

There are two methods of Koran interpretation. The first one consists in explaining the verses and chapters of the Koran, in their traditional order. This may be done from different points of views: grammatical, historical, stylistic, legal and philosophical. However, all these trends in interpretation obscure the Divine Guidance. Often verses are explained in ways completely opposed to their real meanings or purposes and sometimes they are even considered to have been abrogated. According to this traditional method, verses are interpreted on the basis of certain extra-Koranic assumptions or principles. One can see the result e.g. in the exegesis of the verses concerning fighting: about 70 verses are considered to have been abrogated, since they are incompatible with the legitimacy of fighting. Therefore this method of interpretation does scant justice to the fact that the Koran is the primary source of Islam. Moreover, the numerous different interpretations, which were the consequence of this method, created an intellectual anarchy and an aversion against the Koran and its interpreters.

The second method consists in collecting all the verses concerning a certain topic and analyzing then in their interrelation. Thus, the purpose of these verses and the rules that can be derived from them, become clear. There is no need to squeeze any verse into an unsuitable interpretation. Thus, justice is done to all the merits of the Divine Formulation. This second method is, in our view, the exemplary method of Koran-interpretation. It can promote the guidance of humanity as it shows that the Koranic topics are not merely theoretical, but that they also contain realistic examples that are directly relevant to everyday life. Nowadays the false notion is widespread that the Koran is just a spiritual book, only concerned with man's relation to God without any bearing on the practical exigencies of daily life. As a result many people, and among them even those who call themselves scholars, regard the Koran merely as a collection of texts for recitation in order to invoke Allah's protection or to seek recovery from illness. In this way, however, they undervalue the Koran and, in doing so, deprive themselves of an abundant source of knowledge, wisdom, legislation, politics, education and culture.

I applied this second method to the subject: "*The Koran and Women*". The topic I should like to discuss now is "*The Koran and Fighting*". This topic is of practical importance in our times, as wars are being fought all over the world, engaging everybody's attention. Moreover, it has a theoretical significance, as many adherents of other religions constantly take up this subject with a view to discredit Islam. Therefore, people would do well to learn the Koranic rules with regard to fighting, its causes and its ends, and so came to recognize the wisdom of the Koran in this respect: its desire for peace and its aversion against bloodshed and killing for the sake of the vanities of this world and out of sheer greediness and lust.

2. The Nature of the Islamic Mission (*da'wah*)

A first requirement for the treatment of this topic is some knowledge of the nature of the Islamic Mission and an answer to the question whether this Mission needs to force people to conversion.

Sometimes when a man is invited to adopt a certain principle, he can readily do so and believe in it, peacefully and joyfully. However, other principles may be difficult to accept and repulsive to him. We see both phenomena around us and we know them in ourselves. What then is the reason?

The reason is clear. Whenever the truth one is invited to accept is a simple and easy one, not complicated or unnatural and not manifestly or secretly containing elements opposed to human nature, it is clear truth that speaks for itself and does not require any further means to enlist adherents. However, when the truth is contradictory, complicated and intricate, it is dim, obscure and repulsive to people. In order to make people accept such truths, special means are required — they have to be imposed on the people by force. If this is an established fact with regard to the human mind, let us now consider to which of these two categories the Islamic Mission belongs.

Allah sent Mohammed at an interval amongst the messengers, as a caller, a bringer of good tidings and as a warner [cf. K 5:19]. He revealed to him a book containing the principles of happiness for the community as well as for the individual: it commands to judge by reason, it attaches great importance to evidence, it propagates science and knowledge, it gives clear rules, it specifies crimes, it proclaims mercy, it urges to do good, it preaches peace, it puts an end to distress and strives for facility, it gives firm principles concerning politics and society, it fights injustice and corruption, it struggles against mental sluggishness, it disapproves of blind imitation of the ways of the forefathers, it shouts at people that another life more exalted than this life, is awaiting then and will offer them permanent bliss and eternal existence and that Man ends where he begins and that his life in the Hereafter will be determined by his life in this world.

Thus was the Mission of Mohammed, the messenger. Its foremost principle was the unity of the Creator and the worship only of him, and belief in him, free from defective and imperfect qualities or of any characteristic that can be compared with His creation: "*Originator of the heavens and the earth, how shall He have offspring, seeing He has had no female companion, and has created everything? He everything doth know. That is Allah your Lord, there is no god but He, the creator of everything, so serve Him; He of everything hath charge. Sight reacheth not to Him, but He is able to reach the sight; He is the Gentle, the Well-informed*" (K 6:101-3).

The Koran points out that thus it wants to honour Man and seeks to keep him from worshipping something that does not see nor hear and that is neither harmful nor beneficial. It announces that by this message the previous religions are confirmed, that it is not opposed to their original principles and that it does not discriminate between the different Messengers: they all proclaim the unity of God, they all require the worship of God, they all command to do what is good and forbid to do what is reprehensible and they all recommand virtue and preach against evil:

"*Say ye: 'We have believed in Allah and what has been sent down to us, and what has been sent down to Abraham and Ishmael and Isaac and Jacob and the Patriarchs and what has been given to Moses and Jesus and what has been given to the prophets from their Lord, making no distinction between any of them; and to Him are we submissive. So if they believe in something like what ye believe in, they have been guided; but if they turn away, it is they who are in schism; Allah will attend to them for thee, He is the one who hears and knows*' " (K 2:136-7).

"*Say*: '*O People of the Book, come to a word* (*which is*) *fair between us and you,* (*to wit*) *that we serve no one but Allah, that we associate nothing with Him, and that we do not take one the other as Lords apart from Allah*'; *if then they turn away, say ye*: "*Bear witness that we are Moslems*' " (K 3:64).

"*Dispute ye not with the People of the Book except with what is better, unless it be those of them who have done wrong, and say*: '*We believe in what has been sent down to us and sent down to you*; *our God and your God are one, and we to Him are surrenderers* (*of ourselves*)' " (K 29:46).

"*He hath made accessible for you in religion what He laid as a charge upon Noah and that which We have suggested to thee, and what We laid as a charge upon Abraham and Moses and Jesus* (*saying*): '*Establish the religion and do not divide into parties regarding it*' " (K 42:13).

As these and other verses with regard to the Islamic Mission show, this Mission is a clear and evident one, easy and uncomplicated, not obscure and abstruse, but digestible and intelligible for any mind. It is identical with the Mission of previous religions, the Mission of former Messengers. It is the call of natural reason and therefore not alien to human intellect: "*The savour of Allah, Who is better in savour*..." (K 2:138); "*The natural religion laid down by Allah which He hath formed the people by nature to follow, there is no alteration of the creation of Allah. That is the right religion...*" (K 30:30). Such is the Mission of Islam. Now, does such a Mission require force to make people believe in it? No, the use of force as a means of making people believe in this Mission, would be an insult to it, would make it revolting and would put obstacles in its way. If a man realizes that he is being compelled, or forced into something, this will prevent him from respecting and esteeming it and from reflecting upon it, let alone that he will be able to believe in it. Employing force as an instrument for conversion means wrapping this Mission in complexity, absurdity and obscurity and withholding it from the grasp of the human mind and heart. This, without doubt, would be a terrible injustice to this Mission as well as an insult and at the same time it would stand as an obstacle in its way. It would be incomprehensible for a Mission to pursue its aims while containing in itself elements conducive to its weakness and ultimate extinction or components that are harmful to it and distort its beauty. All this is clear and we could leave it at that, confident that people will respect it and take it as a guiding principle in their judgement concerning the relationship between Islam and fighting. However, we shall not content ourselves with this; we shall examine the texts referring to the Mission and investigate whether there are any texts that approve of coercion in matters of faith and whether there are any texts that express regard for faith based on compulsion. The answer should be evident, and from several points of view at that.

The Koran instructs us clearly that Allah did not wish people to become believers by way of force and compulsion, but only by way of study, reflection and contemplation. Moreover, the Koran teaches us that, had He wanted them to have such a kind of faith, He would have implanted it in their nature and made them like angels, unable to disobey His orders, performing what He orders them to do by nature and creation, powerless to rebel against Him or to escape from Him. However, He did not do so and He left Man free to choose between belief and unbelief, between guidance and going astray. Instead, He contented Himself with their pledges of the natural religion, making them confirm these pledges with regard to themselves and sending prophets to them to remind them and to summon them to think about the kingdom of heaven and earth, "*so that people should have no argument against Allah after* (*the coming of*) *messengers*" (K 4:165); "*lest ye should say*: '*Neither bringer of good tidings nor warner has come to us*' " (K 5:19). Such is the custom of Allah as related in His Book: "*If thy Lord had so pleased He would have made the people one community*; *but they go on differing, except those upon whom thy Lord had mercy*; *for that He created them*" (K 11:118). "*If thy Lord so willed, all those in the land would believe in a body*; *wilt thou then put constraint upon the people that they may be believers?*" (K 10:99). "*Had Allah so willed, He would have made you one community, but* (*He hath not done so*) *in order that He might try you in regard to what has come to you*; *so strive to be foremost in what is good*; *it is to Allah that ye return, all of you, and He will announce to you in which ye have been differing*" (K 5:48). "*If their turning away is a great thing to thee, then if thou art able to seek a hole in the earth or a ladder to the heaven, so as to bring them a sign... But if Allah had so willed He would have gathered them to the guidance*; *so be not thou one of the ignorant*" (K 6:35).

Upon this principle of creation the Divine Revelations are founded: they demand profession of the unity of God and the sole worship of the Creator on the basis of investigation, demonstration, and free choice, proceeding on the principle that there is no power but reason and no coercion except force of argument. You will find that none of the Divine Revelations does impose convictions upon people by way of force and compulsion. Listen to what Nūḥ (Noah) said to his people: "*He said: 'O my people, have ye considered — if I stand upon a Evidence from my Lord, and He hath bestowed upon me a mercy from Himself, and it has been withheld from your sight, shall we cause you to adhere to it, though ye be to it averse?'* " (K 11:28). Then listen to what the people of 'Ād said to their prophet: "*They said: 'O Hūd, thou hast not brought us an Evidence, and we are not going to desert our gods at thy word; nor are we going to give thee credence.'* " (K 11:53). Thereupon he answers: "*Verily I have set my trust upon Allah, my Lord and your Lord, there is not a beast but He takes it by the forelock; verily my Lord is upon a straight path*" (K 11:56). Listen also to Ibrāhīm (Abraham) where he tries to convince his father in a friendly and gently manner, by way of arguments and evidence, emotion and affection:

" *'O my father, verily there has come to me knowledge which has not come to thee; so follow me, and I shall guide thee a path, smooth. O my father, serve not Satan, verily Satan has become to the Merciful an opponent. O my father, verily I fear lest punishment from the Merciful may touch thee and thou become to Satan a client' He said: 'Art thou averse to my gods, O Abraham? If thou dost not refrain I shall surely stone thee; avoid me for a long time'. He said: 'Peace be upon thee! I shall ask pardon for thee of my Lord; verily He hath been with me condescending. And I shall withdraw from you, and from what ye call upon apart from Allah, and I shall call upon my Lord; it may be that I shall not be in my calling upon my Lord unfortunate*' " (K 19:43-7). Listen finally to what Allah says to Mūsa (Mozes) and Hārūn (Aaron) when he entrusted then with the task to spread His Mission : "*Go to Pharaoh, he has become arrogant, and speak to him gently, mayhap he will take heed or fear*" (K 20:43). Read all this very carefully, and then you will know that the only weapons Allah has given to his previous messenger in order to communicate His Mission to the people, were clear arguments and calling the attention to Allah's works. This is entirely in accordance with His custom concerning belief and unbelief, guidance and going astray.

All this Allah has told to His Prophet in His book. He explained to him how the messengers were propagating His Mission and He said to him : "*These are they whom Allah hath guided, so copy* (*thou*) *their guidance*" (K 6:90). Then He explained to him the methods of propagating the message in one unique and comprehensive verse : "*Summon to the way of thy Lord with wisdom and goodly admonition and argue against them with what is better*" (K 16:125). This is the principle upon which Mohammad's Mission was founded : "*Say* : '*This is my way — I summon to Allah on the basis of a Demonstration, I and those who follow me. Glory be to Allah, I am not one of those who associate* (*others with Him*)' " (K 12:108). The above-mentioned is characteristic for Mohammed's Mission as well as the Missions of his brethren who preceded him. However, there is one quality with which Allah exclusively endowed Mohammed's Revelation. In his Mission, He made him the prophet who was the least inclined to use compulsion and to employ special expedients for making people believe. The Mission of former prophets had frequently been accompanied by apparent miracles, inducing people to conversion, such as revivication of the dead, and healing of the blind and the leprous. But with regard to Mohammed's revelation Allah refused to conform to the desires of the heathens who demanded that he should give such tokens: "*They say: 'We shall not give thee credence till thou causest for us to bubble up from the earth a spring; Or until thou hast a garden of palm and vine, and thou cause in the midst of it rivers to gush forth; Or until thou causest the heaven to fall upon us in fragments as thou hast said, or thou producest Allah and the angels assenting. Or until thou hast a house of ornamental work, or thou ascendest into the heaven, nor shall we give credence to thy ascent until thou bringest down to us a writing which we may read'. Say: 'Glory be to my Lord! am I anything but a human being (sent) as a messenger?'*" (K 17:90-3).

He explained that his only token was of the same kind as his clear Mission: based on rational demonstration that affects insight rather than eyesight and that takes hold of the heart before it takes hold of the outward senses: "*They say: 'Why are not signs from his Lord sent down to him?' Say: 'Signs are with Allah only and I am only a warner clear'. Hath is not sufficed them that We have sent down to thee the Book to be recited to them? Surely in that is a mercy and a reminder to a people who believe. Say: 'Allah sufficeth as a witness between you and me; He knoweth what is in the heavens and the earth, and those who have believed in what is vain and have disbelieved in Allah — they are the losers'*" (K 29:50-2). "*If We (so) please, We shall send down upon them from the heaven a sign, and their necks will become to it submissive*" (K 26:4).

With these and similar verses of which there are many to be found in the Koran, Allah explains that the Koran itself is sufficient to make people believe in Mohammed's

Mission and that He does not want to force them by means of awe-inspiring tokens. On the other hand He explains that the task of the Messenger amongst them is no more than to communicate his Mission, to admonish and to announce good tidings, a task that Allah has laid down in the Meccan part of the Koran, dating from the period that the Moslems were few in number and without any power, as well as in the Medinan part, dating from the period that the Moslems had acquired considerable strenght and fortitude. To the Meccan part belong the following verses: "*It is nothing less than a Reminder to the worlds*; *To whoever of you wills to act straight*" (K 81:27-8). "*So warn*; *thou art indeed a warner, But thou art not over them an overseer*; *Except* (*over*) *him who turns away and disbelieves*; *Him Allah will punish with the greatest punishment*; *Verily it is to Us that they resort*; *And it rests upon Us with them to reckon*" (K 88:21-6).

To the Medinan part belongs this verse: "*Say*: '*Obey Allay and obey the messenger*; *if then ye turn away, there only rests upon him what has been laid upon him, and upon you what has been laid upon you, but if ye obey him ye will be guided*; *all that rests upon the messenger is the clear proclamation*' " (K 24:54).

There are many similar verses confirming and supporting this, explaining the task of the Messenger and his function in propagating Allah's religion. How remote all this is from the smell of compulsion! How strong is its aversion from the use of force as a means of propagating the Mission. Moreover, the Koran states clearly and distinctly that faith produced by force is without value and that he who yields to force and changes his faith loses his honour. He replied to Firʿawn (Pharaoh) when he was on the point of drowning and said: "*I believe that there is no god but He whom the Children of Israel have believed in*". "*Now! Though formerly thou didst oppose and wast one of those who caused corruption!*" (K 10:90-1). "*Then when they saw Our prowess, they said: 'We believe in Allah alone, and we disbelieve in what with Him we have been associating'*". *But their belief when they saw Our prowess did not benefit them — the custom of Allah seen in the past with regard to His servants; there will lose the unbelievers*" (K 40:84-5).

In the same way the Koran states that repentance cannot be accepted if it has been aroused by coercion or by imminent chastisement. "*The relenting is not in favour of those who go on committing evil deeds until when one of them is in the very presence of death he says: 'I repent now!'*" (K 4:18).

When the Koran asserts, as you see, the futility of faith and repentance aroused by coercion, not having freely and peacefully been accepted by the heart, how then could anyone infer that the Koran would require or enforce coercion in matters of religion, regardless of which religion is concerned? "*There is no compulsion in religion; rectitude has become clearly distinguished from perversity, so whoever disbelieves in Tāghūt and believes in Allah has laid hold upon the firmest handgrip which never gives way; Allah is one who hears and knows*" (K 2:256).

The foregoing has proved that there is absolutely no justification for anybody, whoever it may be, to hold or profess that one of the ways in which the Mission of Islam has been propagated, has been conversion by means of the sword or by fighting. We can summarize this chapter in the following conclusions:

1. In the nature of the Islamic Mission there is no complexity,

obscurity or unintellegibility that would require the use of manifest or secret compulsion.*

2. The Islamic legislation, on the strength of the Book of Allah, is not in conflict with Allah's principle of creation, which accounts for the fact that some people belief whereas others do not. This principle consists in leaving people free to choose for themselves on the basis of examination and conviction.
3. The Islamic Legislation, also on the strength of the Book of Allah, rejects, in plain and unambiguous words, the use of compulsion as a means to propagate religion, as do the previous legislations.
4. The Prophet of Islam was responsible towards his Lord only in so far as his missionary task was concerned. This task has been expounded in both the Meccan and the Medinan parts of the Koran. It consisted in communicating the Mission and admonition. He was not responsible for the conversion of people, which might have induced compulsion and the use of force.**
5. Allah's Book, the source of the Islamic Mission, does not respect faith brought about by compulsion, and it denies its having any consequence on the Day of Resurrection. How then can it enjoin compulsion or allow the use of it as a means to conversion?

One may find these conclusions in the Koran itself. Believing in them is part of believing in the Koran. This

---

* (Note by Shaltūt): By manifest compulsion is meant compulsion by physical force like iron or fire; by secret compulsion is meant compulsion produced by perceptible miracles to which one submits.

** (Note by Shaltūt:) This was different from his responsibility or that of the Caliphs in applying his legislation on his community.

being established, one may now ask : Given these conclusions of which the Koran speaks, what then is the significance of the verses of fighting in the Koran?

This will be our second topic.

3. The Verses of Fighting

In this chapter we shall expound the Verses of Fighting in the Koran, in order to understand their meaning and purpose and to learn their relation to one another. After that we shall arrive at a conclusion which, together with the conclusions reached in the preceding chapter, will elucidate those verses that order fighting.

The Koran is concerned with two kinds of fighting : the fighting of Moslems against Moslems and the fighting of Moslems against non-Moslems.

The first kind belongs to the internal affairs of the Islamic state (*ummah*) and concerns only this state with the exclusion of any other state. The Koran deals with the event of rebellion and breach of public order, either between two groups of subjects or between subjects and rulers. It gives certain provisions for this event with a view to preserve the unity of the Islamic state (*ummah*) and the power of and the respect for the ruling class, and to protect the community against the evils of rebellion and mutual hostility. These provisions are to be found in *Sūrat al-Ḥudjurāt* : "*If two parties of the believers fight, set things right between them, and if one of the two parties oppress the other, fight the one which is oppressive until it returns to the affair of Allah; then if it returns, set things right between them justly, and act fairly; verily Allah loveth those who act fairly.*

The believers are brethren, set things right therefore between your two brethren, and show piety towards Allah; mayhap ye will have mercy shown you" (K 49:9-10).

This verse assumes a case of disagreement between two groups of believers that cannot be solved by peaceful means, so that both groups resort to the use of force and leave the final decision to the sword. In this case it prescribes, that the Islamic state (*ummah*), represented by its government, investigate the causes of discord and endeavour to set things right between the parties. If this can be attained by means of negotiations, and both parties obtain what is due to them so that rebellion is warded off and safety and peace prevail, then Allah saves the believers the trouble of fighting. However, if one of the parties continues to oppress the other, refuses to return to the affair of Allah and attacks the authority of the believers, then they have become rebels against the legal power and public order. In that case the community of Moslems is obliged to fight them until they submit and return to what is right. Further, this verse points out the secret of success in solving discord arising between different groups. This secret is that the return of one of the parties to what is right, should not be used as a means to oppress them or to deprive them of their rights. Instead, justice must prevail and each party must have its due. Consider the end of the verse (K 49:9): "*Verily, Allah loveth those who act fairly*". Furthermore the second verse teaches that what these provisions aim at is to preserve the unity and undivisibility of the Islamic state and to safeguard the religious brotherhood which is one of the most important matters of faith, for it reads: "*The believers are brethern, set things right therefore between your two brethern, and show piety towards Allah; mayhap ye will have mercy shown you*" (K 49:10).

These wise Koranic provisions were revealed by the mouth of the illitterate [59] Prophet, as instruments to secure peace and in order to exterminate rebellion and aggression, more than thirteen centuries before the human mind invented what is called the "League of Nations" or the "Security Council" to serve as a means of preservation of peace, consolidation of liberties and enjoyment by all states of their rights.

Had the nations understood these wise provisions with true understanding, had they given them the attention they deserve and had they followed their purport, then these nations would never have gone astray from the path of wisdom and they would have been saved from the frequent disasters caused by rebellion and aggression on the one hand and disagreement and discord on the other.

These are the rules the Koran gives with regard to fighting between Moslems. It is evident that they bear no relation whatsoever to the principles of the Islamic Mission and faith.

The second kind of fighting, viz. fighting between Moslems and non-Moslems, has been dealt with comprehensively in many Koranic verses and chapters. The Koran goes into the causes which may lead to it, its aim, upon the attainment of which fighting must stop, the obligatory preparations for it by the Moslems and the necessary caution against an unexpected outbreak of it. It treats of many provisions and regulations and enters upon connected subjects like armistices or treaties. In the following we shall discuss the verses dealing with the cause of fighting, and with the aim of fighting, upon the attainment of which the fighting must stop and finally we shall go into the relation between the Verses of Forgiveness and the Verses of Fighting.

In Mecca, the Moslems suffered for several years under the

worst kinds of punishment, oppressed in their religious freedom, persecuted for the sake of the creed in which they found reassurance and terrorized with regard to property and personal safety. For all these reasons they were compelled to emigrate. They left their dwellings and settled in Medina, patiently submitting to Allah's orders and gladly accepting His authority. Whenever they felt the urge to resist the oppression and to revenge themselves on the oppressors, the Prophet held them back, bidding them to be patient in expectation of a command from Allah. "I have not been ordered to fight" he used to say. This lasted so long that they were almost overcome by desperation, and consequently by doubts and misgivings. And just then Allah revealed the first verses of fighting: "*Permission is granted to those who are fought because they have suffered wrong; verily to help them Allah is able.*[60] *Who have been expelled from their dwellings without justification, except that they say: 'Our Lord is Allah'. But for Allah's warding off the people, some by means of others, hermitages and churches and oratories and places or worship in which the name of Allah was had in remembrance would have been destroyed in numbers. Surely Allah will help those who help Him; Allah is strong, sublime. Who, if We establish them in the land, will observe the Prayer, and pay the Zakāt, urge to what is reputable and restrain from what is disreputable — to Allah belongs the issue of affairs*" (K 22:39-41). These verses deal with the permission to fight. This permission was motivated by the fact that the Moslems suffered injustice and were forced to emigrate and to leave their dwellings without justification.

They then explain that this permission corresponds with the customary practice that people ward each other off so that a certain equilibrium is attained, oppression is averted,

K 22:39-41 Pilligrimage

and adherents of the different creeds and cults can perform their religious observances and keep believing in the pure doctrine of monotheism. Finally these verses point out that Allah only helps those who help and fear Him and therefore do not use war as an instrument for destruction and corruption, for subjecting the weak and satisfying their own desires and lust, but cultivate the land when it falls into their hands, obey Allah's orders and summon people to do what is good and reputable and not to what is desreputable and wicked. Allah distinguishes between those who act destructively and those who act constructively: "*To Allah belongs the issue of the affairs*" (K 22:41 *in fine*). These verses are, as we have said, the first Verses of Fighting. They are very clear and do not contain even the slighest evidence of religious compulsion. On the contrary, they confirm that the practice that people ward each other off is one of Allah's principles of creation, inevitable for the preservation of order and for the continuation of righteousness and civilization. Were it not for this principle, the earth would have been ruined and all the different places of worship would have been destroyed. This would have happened if powerful tyrants would have held sway over religions, free to abuse them without restraint and to force people to conversion, without anyone to interfere. These verses are not only concerned with Moslems, but have clearly a general impact: "... *hermitages and churches and oratories and places of worship... would have been destroyed...*" (K 22:40).

Let us now have a look at the Verses of Fighting that are to be found in *Sūrat al-Baqarah*: "*Fight in the way of Allah those who fight you, but do not provoke hostility; verily Allah loveth not those who provoke hostility. Slay them wherever ye come upon them and expel them from whence they have expelled you; persecution is worse than slaughter; do not fight them, however, in the precincts of the Sacred Mosque, until they fight you therein, but if they fight you slay them; such is the recompence of the unbelievers. But if they refrain (from fighting) then Allah is forgiving, compassionate. Fight them until there is no persecution and religion becomes Allah's; then if they refrain, let there be no enmity except against the wrong-doers. The sacred month for the sacred month, things sacred being (subject of the law of) retaliation; so if anyone make an attack upon you, make alike attack upon them; show piety towards Allah, and know that Allah is with those who show piety"* (K 2:190-4).

These verses order the Moslems to fight in the way of Allah [61] those who fight them, to pursue them wherever they find them and to scatter them just as they had once scattered the Moslems. They prohibite the provocation of hostility and this prohibition is reinforced by Allah's repugnance to aggression and by his dislike of those who provoke hostility. Then they point out that expelling people from their homes, frightening them while they are safe and preventing them from living peacefully without fear for their lives or possessions is persecution worse than persecution by means of murder and bloodshed. Therefore those who practise or provoke these things must be fought just like those who actually fight. These verses also prohibit fighting in holy places or in holy periods, unless the Moslems are under attack. For if their sacred protection is violated and fighting becomes lawful for them, they are allowed to meet the hostility by the same means by way of retaliation. These points having been explained, the verses finally define the aim upon the attainment of which the war must end. This aim is accomplished when there is no more persecution in matters of religion, and religion is Allah's [cf. K 2:193 and 8:39], so that people obtain religious freedom and are not oppressed or tortured, because of their religion. As soon as this aim has been accomplished and people feel safe, fighting must cease.

In these verses and the principle they contain with regard to the reason and the aim of fighting, there is not a single trace to be found of any idea of conversion by force. On the contrary, these verses, like the previous ones, say in plain and distinct words that the reason for which the Moslems have been ordered to fight is the aggression directed against them, expulsion from their dwellings, violation of Allah's sacred institutions and attempts to persecute people for what they believe. At the same time they say that the aim upon the attainment of which Moslems must cease fighting is the termination of the aggression and the establishment of religious liberty devoted to Allah and free from any pressure or force.

The principles expounded in these verses can be found, in the same or similar words, in many other verses of fighting, e.g. in *Sūrat al-Nisā'*, *Sūrat al-Anfāl* and *Sūrat al-Tawbah*: "*What is wrong with you that ye fight not in the way of Allah and the oppressed, men, women, and children, who say: 'O our Lord, take us out of this city of wrong-doing people, and appoint for us from Thine own side a patron, and appoint for us from Thine own side a helper?'*" (K 4:75). "*So fight thou in the way of Allah, thou art responsible for none but thyself, but urge on the believers; possibly Allah will restrain the martial ardour of those who have disbelieved; Allah is stronger both in martial ardour and in chastisement*" (K 4:84). "*If then they withdraw from you, and do not fight against you, but offer you peace, Allah hath not opened for you a way*

K 4:75

against them. If they do not withdraw from you, and offer you peace, and restrain their hands, take them and kill them wherever ye come upon them" (K 4:90-1).

Read these verses and have a closer look at the following phrases: "*Possibly Allah will restrain the martial ardour of those who have disbelieved*" and "*If they do not withdraw from you...*", then you will realize the spirit of persecution that the people harboured against the Moslems and on account of which the Moslems were ordered to fight. This is exactly the same principle as that which has been expounded in *Sūrat al-Baqarah*, as we have seen, and we will find this principle also in *Sūrat al-Anfāl*: "*Fight them until there is no persecution and the religion is entirely Allah's; if they desist, Allah of what they do is observant*" (K 8:39) and in *Sūrat al-Tawbah*: "*But if they violate their oaths after they have made a covenant and attack your religion, fight the leaders of unbelief; no oath will hold in their case; mayhap they will refrain. Will ye not fight against a people who have violated their oaths, and had it in mind to expel the messenger, and who took the initiative with you the first time? Are ye afraid of them? It is more in order that ye should be afraid of Allah, if ye be believers*" (K 9:13-4). And: "*But fight the polytheists continuously, as they fight you continuously, and know that Allah is with those who act piously*" (K 9:36 *in fine*). Read these verses and consider firstly the phrase: "*But if they violate their oaths after they have made a covenant and attack you religion*", then the phrase: "... *and who took the initiative with you the first time*..." and finally the phrase: "... *as they fight you continuously*..." then you will realize that these verses were revealed with regard to people recalcitrantly practising persecution, amongst whom the elements of depravation were so deeply rooted that they did not respect pledges anymore and that virtue became meaningless to them. There is no doubt that to fight these people, to purify the earth from them and to put an end to their persecution, is to serve the commonweal and a benefaction to mankind as a whole.

After the aforementioned verses, we find in *Sūrat al-Tawbah* two verses which, at first sight, seem to contain prescriptions contradicting the just mentioned principles concerning fighting. We shall quote them here and reveal their true meaning in the light of the previous verses which, because of their frequency and unequivocalness, must be considered fundamental with regard to the legality of fighting and the reasons for it. Therefore, other verses should be compared with the principles they contain and interpreted accordingly.

The first verse reads: "*Fight against those who do not believe in Allah nor in the Last Day and do not make forbidden what Allah and His messenger have made forbidden, and do not practise the religion of truth of those who have been given the book, until they pay the jizya off-hand, being subdued*" (K 9:29). The second one goes: "*O ye who have believed, fight the unbelievers who are near to you, and let them feel a rough temper in you, and know that Allah is with those who show piety*" (K 9:123). The first verse commands the Moslems to fight a certain group which is characterized by the fact that "*they do not believe in Allah etc.*". Previously they had broken their pledges and hindered and assailed the propagation of the Islamic Mission [cf. K 9:7-16]. These acts constitute for the Moslems reasons for fighting them. Therefore this verse does not say that the quality of being an unbeliever etc. constitutes a sufficient reason for fighting, but mentions the characteristics peculiar to them in order to give a factual description and as a further incitement to attack them once their aggression will have materialized. They modified the religion of Allah and took their scholars and monks for Lords apart from Him [cf. K 9:30], while making things allowed and forbidden according to their whims, since they did not accept that only Allah can do so. There was nothing to hold them back from breaking pledges, and violating rights, and they were not inclined to desist from aggression and tyranny.

These are the people which, according to this verse, must be fought continuously until, by being thoroughly subjected, they can do no more harm and will desist from the persecution they used to practise. The Koran introduced a special token for this submission, viz. the payment of poll-tax (*djizyah*), which means that they actually participate in carrying the burdens of the state and providing the means for the common-weal, both for Moslems and non-Moslems.*

* (Note by Shaltūt:) Poll-tax (*djizyah*) is not, as some people think, a sum paid in return for the right to refuse conversion to Islam or in return for their lives. It is, as we have said, a symbol for their submission and for their desistance from fighting and impeding the Islamic Mission, and a token of their participation in the affairs of the state, which grants them protection of their lives and property. Abū Yūsuf[62] mentioned in his *Kitāb al-Kharādj*, p. 35: "After Abū 'Ubaydah[63] had concluded a peace treaty with the people of Syria and had collected poll-tax (*djizyah*) and land-tax (*kharādj*) from them, he was informed that the Byzantines were raising troups against him and that the situation had become critical for him and the Moslems. He then wrote to the governors of those cities with which a treaty had been concluded that they must return the poll-tax (*djizyah*) and the land-tax (*kharādj*) they had collected and say to them: "We return to you your property since we have been informed that troops are being raised against

Two phrases in this verse indicate the reason for fighting which we have already pointed out. These phrases are: "*being subdued*" and "*off-hand*". They determine the state wherein they will come when poll-tax (*djizyah*) is collected from them, viz. a state of submission to the authority of the Moslems and subjection to their laws. There is no doubt that this implies that previously they had been recalcitrant and that there had been reasons for the Moslems to fight them. This is how this verse is to be understood. This interpretation is supported by the context and brings this verse in agreement with the other verses. For if this verse had meant that they must be fought because of their unbelief and that unbelief had been the reason why they should be fought, then it would have been laid down that the aim of fighting then consisted in their conversion to Islam. Collecting poll-tax (*djizyah*) from them would not have been allowed in that case and they would not have been allowed abide by their own religion.

The second verse: "*... fight the unbelievers who are near to you...*" is not to be compared with the previous verses because those verses indicate the reason and motive for fighting, whereas this verse has been revealed as a directive for a practical war plan, to be followed when legitimate fighting actually breaks out. Thus it informs the Moslems that, when the enemies are manifold, it is imperative to fight the nearest first of all, then the nearest but one and

---

us. You have stipulated that we should protect you, whereas now we are not able to do so. We now return what we have taken from you, but we will abide by the stipulation and what has been written down, if Allah grants us victory over them".

so on, in order to clear the road from enemies and to facilitate the victory.*

This principle, formulated by the Koran, is still being followed today by belligerent states, for attacking states do not advance unless they have cleared the roads before them and are sure that there are no more obstacles in their way. Thus it is clear that these two verses have no link with the reason for fighting, as formulated by the other verses.

From the preceding words one may infer :

1. That there is not a single verse in the Koran which could support the opinion that the aim of fighting in Islam is conversion;

---

* (Note by Shaltūt :) Some people who were bent on disparaging Islam did not go beyond the ostensible interpretation of "... *fight the unbelievers that are near to you*..." and pretended that the Islamic religion ordered to fight the unbelievers in general, regardless of whether they had committed aggression or not, until they had been converted to Islam. They said that this rule was founded on this verse. However, the meaning of the word "unbelievers" in this and similar verses is : "those hostile polytheists who fight the Moslems, commit aggression against them, expel them from their homes and their property and practise persecution for the sake of religion". The morals of these polytheists have been discussed in the opening verses of *Sūrat al-Tawbah*. The word "people" in the tradition : "*I have been ordered to fight the people*" [64] should be understood in the same manner. For according to the Consensus (*idjmā'*), fighting must only cease at what is mentioned in this tradition if the enemies are Arab polytheists.[65] As for other enemies, the war against them must cease on the condition that they "*pay the djizyah off-hand, being subdued*". If this interpretation is accepted, the different verses are in agreement, there is no contradiction left between the Koran and the Tradition and the aforementioned false allegation has been disposed of.

2. That, as explained by the verses mentioned above, there are only three reasons for fighting, viz. to stop aggression, to protect the Mission of Islam and to defend religious freedom;

3. That in giving its prescriptions for fighting, the Koran did not admit of avidity, selfishness and humilation of the poor as motives for it, but intended it as an instrument for peace and tranquillity and for a life founded on justice and equality.

4. That poll-tax (*djizyah*) is not a financial compensation for the granting of one's life or preservation of one's own religion, but a symbol of submission and desistance from harmful acts and a contribution in carrying the burdens of the state.

After this exposé nobody can vilify Islam anymore or misinterpret the Koranic verses and maintain as some ignoramuses have done, that Islam has taken up fighting as a means of propagating its Mission and as an instrument for conversion, and that its Mission and creed were founded on and propagated by suppression and the use of force.

Here we shall cite a verse from *Sūrat al-Mumtaḥinah* which may be considered as an Islamic charter concerning the relations between Moslems and non-Moslems: "*Allah doth not forbid you to act virtuously towards those who have not fought against you in the matter of religion, and have not expelled you from your dwellings, or to deal fairly with them—Allah loveth those who deal fairly*" (K 60:8).

Read this charter and then turn your attention to *Sūrat al-Mā'idah*, one of the parts of the Koran that were revealed most recently. There you may read the following with regard to the relations between Moslems and non-Moslems: "*Today the good things are made allowable for you; the food of those who have been given the Book is allowable for you, and your food is allowable for them; also the women who are under ward of the believers, and the women who are under ward of those who have been given the Book before you, when ye have given them their hires, taking them in ward, neither committing fornication, nor choosing paramours. If anyone disbelieve in the faith his work has gone for nothing and in the Hereafter he will be among the losers*" (K 5:5).

Read all this and you will know the lofty spirit of righteousness, equity, co-operation and affinity that Islam cherishes with regard to its relations with non-Moslems. It is a kind of relationship so magnificent that, compared with it the most modern principle known to the human mind in international relations wanes into insignificance.

4. The Connection between the Verses of Forgiveness and the Verses of Fighting

In this treatise we cannot pass over a problem that has occupied the minds of many people while examining the Koran and comparing its verses. These people fall into two categories:

A group of adversaries of the Religion, who look for arguments against it in the Koran itself.

A group of Koran-interpreters whom religious zeal has driven to harmonize between supposed inconsistencies within the Koran and who are inclined to consider some verses as having abrogated other verses. Some of them let themselves be carried away to such an extent that they seem to have prepared the road, unintentionally, for attacks by adversaries of the Religion. As for the adversaries, they have examined the relations between the different Verses of Fighting and between the Verses of Fighting as a whole and the Verses of Pardon and Forgiveness. They then said: Whereas you see that some verses of fighting only allow fighting, there are others that make it incumbent urge on to it. And whereas you see that some of these verses order to fight aggressors and forbid to commit aggression, there are other verses that order to fight them all without mercy and clemency and without distinguishing between aggressors and others. And whereas you see that these verses as a whole order to fight and regulate fighting, there are many other verses to be found in all chapters of the Koran, instructing to be forgiving, to counter evil with good and to summon to Allah with wisdom [cf. K 16:125]. All these, allegedly, are inconsistencies incompatible with the fact that the Koran of Mohammed is a divine revelation, disclosed to him by Allah. As for the Koran-interpreters, they hold that the Verses of Fighting have abrogated the Verses of Forgiveness and Pardon, even verses like: "*Good and evil are not on the same footing; repel (the evil) with what is better*" (K 41:34) and "*Summon to the way of thy Lord with wisdom and goodly admonition, and argue against them with what is better*" (K 16:125).

They claim that verse 36 of *Sūrat al-Tawbah* (chapter 9): "*But fight the polytheists continuously as they fight you continuously*" has abrogated the preceding Verses of Forgiveness. One of their most peculiar opinions is that the phrase "*Kill them where ye find them*" in the end of verse 191 of *Sūrat al-Baqarah* (chapter 2) abrogates the immediately preceding one: "*Fight in the way of Allah those who fight you*" and also that verse 193 of the same chapter: "*Fight them until there is no persecution*" abrogates the following words of verse 191: "*Do not fight them, however, in the precincts of the Sacred Mosque, until they fight you therein*".

This pericope, occurring in *Sūrat al-Baqarah* and consisting of four verses, thus becomes a pericope containing two abrogating and two abrogated verses: the second has abrogated the first and the fourth the third. Al-Rāzī [66] has said in his exegesis on the Koran, commenting on this view: "It is improbable that the Wise One brings some verses together in pairs of which one verse abrogates the other". It is not improbable that this interpretation has paved the way for the opinion of the adversaries of the Religion, namely that the Koran is inconsistent. They do not accept the notions of abrogation as claimed by the commentators and how can they accept it from us while even some of our own scholars do not. After this exposé you will probably realize that there is no contradiction or incompatibility between the different verses of fighting and no room for opinions that some of them have been abrogated by others, since abrogation may only be applied when there is a contradiction. These verses are therefore fixed and unassailable. They all amount to the same thing and establish one and the same rule, one and the same reason and one and the same end.

As for the Verses of Forgiveness and Pardon, they are meant to shape morality. They are valid within their own range as long as they do not infringe on pride and honour. As there is a separate legislation for every situation, these verses are also fixed and unassailable.

Legislation based upon consideration for different situations, and for the different conditions of individuals and groups, a legislation that requires of people that they follow in every situation that which is most suitable, cannot be accused of being an inconsistent legislation or of being a legislation of which one part abrogates the other. People with common sense will consider it as a wise and extremely precise legislation that promotes the interest of those who fall under its authority and that will realize its ultimate aim viz. happiness of the individual and the community.

5. The Verses concerning the organisation of Fighting

One of the conclusions arrived at in the first part was that there are only three reasons for fighting, viz. repelling aggression, protecting the Mission of Islam and defending religious freedom. Only in these cases has Allah made fighting lawful and urged on to it. He revealed many prescriptions and rules that guarantee victory. In this chapter we will expound the verses that deal from this angle with fighting.

If one studies these verses of Allah's Book, one will discover that they lay down general principles for the Moslems, constituting a handbook for warfare ranking very high among similar institutions of modern civilization.

A handbook for warfare for a nation that wants to acquire pride and honor, must be based upon three elementary considerations :

1. Strengthening the morale of the nation;
2. Preparation of material force;
3. The practical aspects of warfare.

In outlining how people can live a good life, the Koran also deals with these three elementary considerations. This is done in a manner which comprises everything that human skill has produced in different ages and varying cultures; it is not restricted to one age but leaves room for new institutions and instruments. Powerful and extensive as this method is, it dominates the hearts of the people, fills them with notions of mercy and compassion and provides them with the spirit of loyalty and a desire for Allah's approval in purifying the earth from corruption and clearing it from tyranny and aggression. You will find that these notions are represented in all of these three elements.

The first element, viz. strengthening the morale of the nation.

The Koran says: "*So let those who barter this present life for the Hereafter, fight in the way of Allah; upon whomsoever fights in the way of Allah and is killed or overcomes, We shall in the end bestow a mighty hire. What is wrong with you that ye fight not in the way of Allah and the oppressed, men, women, and children, who say: 'O our Lord, take us out of this city of wrong-doing people, and appoint for us from Thine own side a patron, and appoint for us from Thine own side a helper?' Those who have believed are fighting in the way of Allah, and those who have disbelieved are fighting in the way of Tāghūt, so fight the friends of Satan; verily the craft of Satan has become weak*" (K 4:74-6). These words mobilize the fighting spirit by saying that it is fighting in the way of Allah, who doubles the reward of the human beings and the reward for those who struggle (*mudjāhidūn*); that it is fighting for the sake of the weak, for the sake of righteousness towards one's fellowmen, for the sake of resistance against tyranny and despotism; and that it is fighting to suppress evil and corruption.

The Koran also says: "*Do ye liken the giving of water to the pilgrimage, and the management of the Sacred Mosque to (the conduct) of him who has believed in Allah and the Last Day, and has striven in the cause of Allah? They are not alike in Allah's estimation; Allah guideth not the wrong-doing people. Those who have believed and emigrated and striven with goods and person in the cause of Allah are of higher rank in Allah's estimation; they are the blessed. Their Lord giveth them good tidings of mercy and goodwill from Himself, and Gardens for them in which is enduring delight; in which they will abide for ever; verily with Allah is mighty reward*" (K 9:19-22). Read this verse and repeat it a few times for yourself. Turn your attention to the words: "*Verily with Allah is mighty reward*". Then you will know that for those who struggle in person or with their money in the way of Allah the reward is unlimited, and cannot be comprehended but by the Great Exalted One who knows all things, visible and unvisible.

The Koran also says: "*Allah hath bought from the believers their persons and their goods at the price of the Garden (in store) for them, fighting in the way of Allah and killing and being killed — a promise binding upon Him in the Torah, the Evangel, and the Qur'ān; and who fulfils his covenant better than Allah? So rejoice in the bargain ye have made with Him; that is the mighty bliss*" (K 9:111).

With these words it reminds them of the Divine Promise that He has taken upon Him on behalf of those who struggle on His way. This Promise He has announced in all His Books. Now He presents it in the form of a contract between buyer and seller that implies obligations for both parties. It assures them that in complying with the obligations of this Promise and in sacrifices made in order to keep it, there is ultimate bliss.

Another verse goes: "*Say: 'If your fathers and your sons and your brethren and your wives and your clan, and properties which ye have acquired, and trade which ye fear may grow slack, and dwellings which please you are dearer to you than Allah and His messenger and striving in His cause, then wait until Allah cometh with His affair; Allah guideth not the people who are reprobates*" (K 9:24).

This verse comprises all factors that may lead to cowardice and weakness and it demands that all believers sacrifice themselves on the path of Allah and Truth, for the sake of welfare and happiness. For neither fathers, sons, brethren, wives or clan, nor the properties, which have been paid for with comfort and happiness, nor the trade that he fears to decline or the dwellings that are dear to him, nothing of all this may come between the believer and the sacrifices and struggle that the love for Allah and His Messenger demands of him : "*The believers are those who have believed in Allah and His Messenger, and have not afterwards doubted, but have striven with goods and person in the cause of Allah — these are the ones who speak sincerely*" (K 49:15). Therefore, the true creed consists of believing in Allah and His Messenger with a faith that is above all doubts and uncertainty and requires the sacrifice of one's life and property in the struggle on the way of Allah. In this powerful manner, which often occurs in the Koran, Allah fights the factors of weakness and the attitudes of fear and inspires the souls of the Community with sentiments of courage, sacrifice and contempt for the vanities of this world, in order to attain Truth and its victory.

Just as the Koran, in general, seeks to inspire the souls of the Community with these sentiments, and thus tries to create men that are strong in spirit and heart, it strives especially to inspire with these feelings the souls of the strugglers themselves. Speaking of those strugglers that have attained victory and success in the past, it says : "*How many a small band has, by the permission of Allah, conquered a numerous band? Allah is with those who patiently endure*". *They said* : '*O our Lord, pour out upon us patient endurance, make firm our feet, and help us against the people of unbelievers*'.

So by the permission of Allah they routed them, and David killed Jālut; and Allah gave him the kingship and the Wisdom, and taught him of whatever He would" (K 2:249-51).

And addressing the Prophet and reminding him of his role in encouraging the strugglers, in exhorting them to be audacious and firm, and in assuring them of the existence of Allah in such a way that they could be confident, it says: "(*Recall*) *when thou wert saying to the believers: 'Will it not suffice you that your Lord reinforces you with three thousand of the angels sent down?' 'Ay! If ye endure and act piously, and they come upon you in this very rush of theirs, your Lord will reinforce you with five thousand of the angels, designated'. Allah only set that forth as good news for you, that your hearts thereby might be at peace; Help cometh only from Allah, the Sublime, the Wise*" (K 3:124-6). And also: "*Do not grow faint and grieve, now that ye have the upper hand, if ye be believers. If a hurt affect you, a similar hurt has already affected the enemy; These days We cause to alternate amongst the people and* (*it is*) *in order that Allah may know those who have believed, and may choose martyrs from amongst you; Allah loveth not the wrong-doers; and that Allah may purge those who have believed, and sift out the unbelievers. Or did ye think that ye would enter the Garden without Allah first knowing those of You who strove with all their might, and knowing those who endure?*" (K 3:139-42).

It belittles what may befall them in the way of Allah and instructs them that faith gives an unbending power and an unweakening resolution, that Allah's practice consists in giving alternately success to both parties, but that the ultimate victory belongs to those who are patient: "*But do not be weak in seeking the enemy; if ye are suffering they are suffering as much as ye suffer, and ye have hopes from*

Allah which they have not; Allah hath become knowing, wise" (K 4:104).

These are but few of the many things that can be said regarding the strengthening influence of the Koran on the morale of the Community in general and the strugglers in particular.

The second element, viz. preparation of material power. The Koran says: "*Prepare (ye) for them whatsoever force and cavalry (ribāt khayl) ye are capable of (gathering) to overawe thereby the enemy of Allah and your own...*" (K 8:60), and "*Those who have disbelieved would like that ye should neglect your weapons and your baggage, then they would swoop down upon you at one swoop*" (K 4:102). The first verse points out two things that are very important in the life of nations, force and "*ribāṭ*". Force depends on number and equipment. The word force can be used for all implements of war and transportation and for all kinds of supply. The word "*ribāṭ*" can be used for anything that reinforces frontierposts. This verse also explains how peace and stability are promoted by preparation, because by that the enemy is so frightened that he will not get the idea of taking advantage of some weak spot. As for the second verse, it points out that one has to be on one's guard and take precautions lest the enemy unexpectedly start a surprise attack on them.

Instructions of the Koran concerning the benefit to be derived from iron and factories

In this connection we ought not to miss the opportunity of quoting the following unique and significant verse, which draws attention to the force that can be derived from iron, a force that strengthens the power of the believers, necessary for keeping and preserving their rights. This verse goes: "*We formerly sent Our messengers with the Evidences, and We sent down with them the Book and the Balance, that the people might dispense justice; and We sent down Iron, in which there is violent force and also uses for the People, and (We did so also) in order that Allah might know who would help Him and His messengers in the unseen; verily Allah is strong, sublime*" (K 57:25).

Look how He linked together the Book, the Balance and Iron by the fact that they had all been revealed and how to Iron, by means of which the Balance can stand up and justice can be maintained, he ascribed these two characteristics: violent force and great utility. Think of this and then have a look at what the implements for war at sea, on land and in the air are made of. Is there not iron in all these implements? Then consider the words that follow: "... *in order that Allah might know who would help Him and His messengers in the unseen*" and you will know that the assistance of Allah is granted to those who have subjected the Iron and who have won power and strength from it.

If the Moslems recognize the value of Allah's favour in providing them and all mankind with iron, which He revealed, they should also recognize the favour He bestowed upon Dā'ūd (David) in disclosing to him the ways of using this material. Allah has told us this story in His Book in order that we may derive lessons from it. Read these words in *Sūrat Saba'*: "*We bestowed upon David preference from Us; 'O ye mountains return (praises) with him, and ye birds also'; and We made iron tractable for him: 'Make ample (coats of mail), and weave them closely'* ". And "*Work ye uprightly, verily of what ye do I am observant*" (K 34:10-1). Read then how Allah bestowed favour upon Sulaymān (Solomon), in the verses 12 and 13 of the same chapter: "*And to Solomon* (*We subjected*) *the wind which blew a month's* (*journey*) *in the morning, and a month's* (*journey*) *in the evening and We made the spring of brass to flow for him*; *and* (*We subjected*) *some of the jinn, such as wrought before him by the permission of his Lord*; *but whoever of them swerved from Our command, We caused him to taste of the punishment of the Blaze. To work for him what he willed, temples and images, and bowls like cisterns, and pots, standing firm*: '*Work, O family of David in thankfulness*; *rare among My servants is the thankful*' " (K 34:12-3).*

Here we should quote the words of al-Rāzī in his exegesis of verses 30-33 of *Sūrat Ṣād*: "*We gave to David, Solomon*; *how excellent a servant*! *Verily he was in the habit of resorting* (*to Us*). *When there were displayed before him in the evening the resting steeds, He said*: '*Lo, I have loved the love of good things more than the remembrance of my Lord, until they had disappeared behind the veil. Bring them back to me*'. *Then he began to stroke their legs and their necks*" (K 38:30-3), so that you will know that the use of cavalry (*ribāṭ*) is very ancient and was customary in the oldest civilizations, those with the best equipment and the strongest ideas. Al-Rāzī says: "The use of cavalry (*ribāṭ al-khayl*) had been recommended in their religions, just as it is in the religion of

* (Note by Shaltūt:) This verse informs us that Sulaymān's (Solomon) factories produced palaces and their utensils like bowls and pots, and that they produced images. The word "images" has found many explanations. One of them is that they made them like animals, underneath the throne and that they moved mechanically at the ascent (of the throne). Al-Alūsī[67] has said: "Human skills have attained this amount of strangeness".

Mohammed. Once Sulaymān (Salomon) had to go on a raid. He ordered horses to be brought and put into a gallop. Then he observed that he did not like it because of wordly things or personal profit, but that he liked it because Allah ordered him to do so in order to strengthen his religion. That is the meaning of the words : "... *than the remembrance of my Lord*". Then Sulaymān (Solomon) ordered to put them into a gallop and make them run until they would disappear behind the curtain, i.e. pass out of sight. He then ordered the trainers to lead those horses back to him. When they had returned he began to stroke their legs and their necks. The purpose of this stroking was as follows : 1. to honour the horses and to show how high their rank was, as they belong to the most important helpers in repelling the enemy; 2. to show that in governing and pursuing his policy he humbled himself to such a degree that he himself carried out even the lowest duties; 3. to demonstrate that he was the greatest expert concerning horses, their diseases and their defects, for he was examining them and touching their legs and necks in order to investigate whether there were symptoms of some disease...". Another verse regarding crafts and their usefulness to nations is to be found in the story about Allah's prophet Nūḥ (Noah) : "*Make the Ark under Our eyes and Our suggestions*" (K 11:37). These are life-boats. Just as nations need life-boats, they are also in want of ships for defence and attack, ships for the transportation of merchandise and all other purposes required by the exigencies of progress of the nations. Allah has said : "*He is it who hath subjected the sea to service that from it ye may eat fresh flesh, and bring forth ornaments to wear; one may see the ships ploughing through it (and it is) that ye may seek this bounty, mayhap ye will show gratitude*" (K 16:14).

As long as the Moslems do not occupy themselves with the teachings of their religion and the instruction of their Book, in order to understand and to observe them, they will continue to live a contemptible life full of hardship, deficient in power and strength.*

The third element, viz. the practical aspects of warfare. The Koran deals with the general principles of this topic from numerous angles.

1. Regarding the reasons for exemption from military service the Koran says: "*No blame rests on the frail or upon the sick or upon those who find nothing to contribute, if they are honest to Allah and His messenger*" (K 9:92). Thus it restricts the reasons of exemption to frailty, which may be caused by incapacity or old age, to sickness and to the unability to contribute. The Koran does not include among them the fact that one is a university graduate or student or that one has learnt the Koran by heart, that one has paid a financial compensation, nor that one is the son of a man of authority, be it great or small. All these things have become customary in our days of weakness and decay, contrary to the practice in the days of the Prophet and in the following era. The idea of compiling the Koran had been born by fear lest the knowledge of the Koran should vanish

* (Note by Shaltūt:) As the preparation of force depends on money, many verses insist on spending money in the path of Allah. E.g.: "*Whatever ye contribute in the cause of Allah will be repaid in full and ye will not be wronged*" (K 8:60). This means that it will be repaid in full by means of concentration of your force in your country and conquest of the country of your enemies. Another verse says: "*Contribute in the way of Allah; hand not yourselves over to destruction*" (K 2:195), where destruction means destruction by thrift and avarice regarding national defence.

with the extinction of the reciters (*qurrā'*), for they were the most audacious and intrepid fighters in the war of al-Yamāmah [68] and because of their boldness and courage in storming the ranks of the enemy many of them were killed.

2. Regarding declaration of war, the Koran gives warning against attacking the enemy unawares and gives the following rule: "*If thou fearest treachery at all from any people cast back to them (thy covenant) equally; verily Allah loveth not the treacherous*" (K 8:58). This verse orders to denounce treaties when wickedness is feared from the enemy and prescribes that this denunciation should be clear and explicit lest the Moslems commit treachery, of which Allah disapproves and which He does not accept.

3. As regards the call to jihad, it warns against tardiness and slugghishness: "*O ye who have believed, what is the matter with you? When one says to you: 'March out in the way of Allah, ye are weighed down to the ground; are ye so satisfied with this nearer life as to neglect the Hereafter? The enjoyment of this nearer life is in comparison with the Hereafter only a little thing. If ye do not march out He will inflict upon you a painful punishment, and will substitute (for you) another people; ye will not injure Him at all; Allah over everything hath power'*" (K 9:38-9). It admonishes them that if they are sluggish in answering the call to jihad they will suffer a painful punishment, a punishment that consists in humiliation and subjugation and in the transfer of power and authority to another people.

4. As regards the purging of the army from dissenting and dissatisfied elements it says: "*If they were to go forth with you, they would add to you nothing but unsoundness; they would emphasise the rifts among you desiring to bring sedition upon you, and amongst you are some accustomed to listen to*

them; Allah knowth the wrong-doers. They were desirous of sedition before this and turned things upside down for thee, until the truth came and the affair of Allah gained the upper hand in spite of them. Some of them say: 'Admit me and do not tempt me'; have they not fallen into sedition? Verily Gehenna encompasseth the unbelievers. If something good befalls thee, it annoys them, and if misfortune befalls thee, they say: 'We kept good hold of our affair before', and they turn away rejoicing" (K 9:47-50). And also: "*If they were to find a place of refuge, or holes to sink into or a place to creep into, they would turn aside to it and bolt*" (K 9:57). "*So if Allah bring thee back to a party of them, and they ask permission of thee to go forth, say: 'Ye shall never go forth with me, nor ever fight any enemy with me; ye were content to sit still the first time, so sit still with those who stay behind'*" (K 9:83). And finally: "*They will swear to you in order that ye may be satisfied with them; so if ye are satisfied with them, verily Allah will not be satisfied with the people who are reprobates*" (K 9:96). If you study the verses revealed in connection with the Tabūk-campaign [69] in *Sūrat al-Tawbah* (chapter 9), you will discover the bad characteristics that are evidence of an abominable army and you will find things that deserve special attention during a period of mobilization and preparation of strength in order to obtain victory. Read then in *Sūrat al-Aḥzāb* (chapter 33), verse 12 to 20, from: "*The Hypocrites (al-munāfiqūn) and those in whose hearts is disease were saying...*" until "*... and if they should be amongst you, they would not fight except a little*",[70] in order to know more about the peculiarities of deserters.

5. As regards organizing the mobilization, the Koran points out that mobilization should be in proportion to the needs. If necessity calls for the participation of everybody,

then everybody must set out. If partial participation will do, then it is sufficient for only a part to set out, whereas the rest may continue their normal domestic activities and serve as reserve troops for the army. This principle is to be found in the verse: "*It is not for the believers to march out altogether; so why should not a party from each section march out, in order that they may gain understanding in religion and that they may warn their people when they return to them, mayhap they will beware*" (K 9:123)[71] and in: "*O ye who have believed, take precautions and march out in companies, or march out all in a body*" (K 4:71).

6. As regards the organization of the army and the distribution of its unities over the positions of defence, look at what the prophet did, as it has been related in the verse: "(*Recall*) *when thou didst go forth early from thy household to settle the believers in positions for the battle*" (K 3:121) and consider next: "*Verily Allah loveth those who fight in His way drawn up in ranks, like a building well-compacted*" (K 61:4).

7. As regards the obedience to the supreme command, the observance of battle-order, the avoidance of factors leading to failure and the safeguarding of a strong faith, the Koran says: "*O ye who have believed, when ye meet a* (*hostile*) *party, stand firm, and call Allah frequently to mind, mayhap ye will succeed. Obey Allah and His messenger, and vie not with each other in withdrawing so that ye become fainthearted and your reputation go; but endure patiently, verily Allah is with those who patiently endure*" (K 8:45-6).*

---

* (Note by Shaltūt:) If, in order to unify the nation and to guard it from failure, the imam deems it appropriate to suspend normal public law and to lay down special rules for this situation, it is compulsory for him

8. As regards flight from the battle order, the Koran warns against it and foretells the evil outcome: *"O ye who believed, when ye meet those who have disbelieved moving into battle, turn them not your back. Whosoever turns his back to them, unless it be swerving to a flight or wriggling round to a company, has become liable to anger from Allah, and his resort is Gehenna — a bad destination"* (K 8:15-6).

9. As regards the order of attack when there are numerous enemies, the Koran requires that the nearest be first attacked, then the next nearest and so forth, in order to clear the road for the army from any hostile obstacle: *"O ye who have believed, fight the unbelievers who are near to you, and let them feel a rough temper in you, and know that Allah is with those who show piety"* (K 9:123).

10. As regards military secrets, the Koran warns against divulging them, because it considers this as one of the characteristics of the Hypocrites (*al-munāfiqūn*). It prescribes that secrets must be kept by the supreme command and that believers, if they hear any news, must verify it before they rely on it and act on the strength of it. It says: *"If the Hypocrites and the diseased of heart, and those who cause disturbance in the city do not leave off, We shall assuredly incite thee against them; then they will not neighbour thee in it, except for a little"* (K 33:60); *"O ye who have believed, do not be unfaithful to Allah and the messenger, and be not unfaithful to your trusts when ye know"* (K 8:27); *"When anything comes to them, be it of security or of alarm, they spread it abroad, when, if they were to refer it to the messenger and*

---

to do, since, in this case, it is a means of attaining something that is obligatory. In our times this principle is known as the proclamation of martial law.

those who have the command amongst them, those of them who might investigate it would know it. Had it not been for the bounty and mercy of Allah towards you, ye would have followed Satan, except a few" (K 4:83); and finally: "*O ye who have believed, if a reprobate come to you with a report, be clear (about it)*" (K 49:6).

11. As regards truce and peace treaties, the Koran orders to respond to a call for peace and termination of war if the enemy is inclined to it and if they show signs of sincerity and fidelity: "*If they incline to make peace, incline thou to it, and set thy trust upon Allah; verily He is the Hearer, the Knower. If they intend to outwit thee, then what thou hast to count upon is Allah, who hath aided thee by His help, and by the believers*" (K 8:63-4).

12. As regards captivity and the treatment of prisoners of war, the Koran says: "*It is not for a prophet to have prisoners so as to cause havoc in the land*" (K 8:67).

When the Imam has caused havoc in the land and when the taking of captives has been allowed to him, he may choose between liberating them out of kindness without any ransom or compensation and taking ransom from them, which may consist of property or men. The choice must be made on the basis of what he sees as the common interest. "*So when ye meet those who have disbelieved, let there be slaughter until when ye have made havoc of them, bind them fast, then liberate them out of kindness or in return for ransom*" (K 47:4).

13. As regards treaties and the observance of them, the Koran gives special attention to the observance of treaties, prescribing to pay heed to them and forbidding treason and violation of them. It teaches that the aim of treaties is to replace disorder and war by safety and peace and it warns against using them as an artful means to deprive the other

party of its rights or to oppress the weak. Consider the words of the Exalted in *Sūrat al-Naḥl*: "*Fulfil the covenant of Allah when ye have taken it, and do not violate oaths after their confirmation, and your having set Allah as guarantor over you; assuredly Allah knoweth what ye do. Be not like her who unravelled her thread into untwisted strands after it was strong, regarding your oaths as merely intrigue amongst you that ye may be a community more numerous than another; Allah is simply testing you thereby, and assuredly He will make clear to you on the resurrection-day that in regard to which ye have been differing*" (K 16:91-2).*

14. When the Imam realizes that the Moslems will come to harm on account of treaties and that this harm will exceed the advantages to be gained by observing them, he is obliged to denounce them. This denunciation must be openly declared. Read the words of the Exalted at the beginning of *Sūrat al-Tawbah*: "*And a proclamation from Allah and His messenger to the people on the day of the greatest pilgrimage, that Allah renounces the polytheists, (as does) also His messenger*" (K 9:3).

---

* (Note by Shaltūt:) This verse warns against breach of treaties or the conclusion of them in such a way that not all the parties concerned feel save; for then these parties will remain dependent on force and force is ignorant of peace or justice. It also warns against using them as an artful means to plunder the weak, who are compelled by circumstances to consent to them. History teaches that these treaties are immoral and ill-fated. "*Do not regard your oaths as merely intrigue amongst you, so that a foot slip after it has been set firm, and ye taste evil for having turned (people) aside from the way of Allah, and for you there be (in store) a punishment mighty*" (K 16:94). Compare then the teachings of this verse with the treaties concluded by modern civilized nations, which are sources of calamities to the world. May those endowed with insight take this to heart (cf. K 59:2).

These are the principles concerning the practical aspects of warfare which we were able, in our time, to derive from the verses of the Holy Koran. However, as the treasures of the Holy Koran are never exhausted, Man, whenever he will investigate its significations and examine its meanings, will arrive at something new. The best aid for the understanding of the Holy Koran are current events and historical facts, for they are the best interpreters and the clearest road to comprehension of its purposes and its principles. If one studies the military activities of the Prophet contained in it, one will grasp many of these purposes and principles. This will strengthen the believers in their conviction that the Koran is nothing but a revelation, revealed by the Creator of all powers who is cognizant of the intentions of the souls.

6. The practical application of the Koranic prescriptions concerning Fighting

In this epilogue we shall present the practical application of the principles expounded by the Koran, during the epoch of the Prophet and his two Successors, Abū Bakr and 'Umar. Later the Moslems were afflicted by internal and external events that prevented them from observing Allah's prescriptions and laws and compelled them, especially where fighting was concerned, to adopt a practice of a much wider range than that which Allah had prescribed for the jihad in His way.

The stages in the lives of the Prophet and the believers who were with him, are the following:

1. The secret Mission, which a small group of people

believed in. They were associated with the Prophet by close ties of family relationship or friendship, which revealed to them the sublime spirit and the excellent character of the Prophet.

2. The public Mission directed to his clan and then to all mankind.

3. The period of negotiations during which the Meccans tried to tempt the Prophet to desist from propagating his Message in exchange for as much property, power and sovereignty as he wished.

4. The period of violence and oppression. History has recorded bloodcurdling instances of torture.

5. The period of Emigration to Ethiopia in order to save the Religion and to rescue lives.

6. The period of artful tricks and plots and conspirations against the Prophet, the Moslems and even against all Banū ʿAbd Manāf [72] in order to prompt the latter to deliver the Messenger and his companions. and not to protect them from the aggression of the Polytheists. One of these actions was the boycott of the people of Abū Ṭālib,[73] which had grave consequences for the Moslems and which — were it not for the affair of Allah — nearly broke their spirit of resistance.

7. The period of seeking refuge in al-Ṭā'if, where Thaqīf [74] was asked for help, who then met the Prophet and his company with mockery and derision and drove them back to where they came from.

8. The period of the Emigration (*Hidjrah*) to Medina. This had been prepared for by delegations that had visited the Prophet and by the pains taken by him to explain the Mission to the tribes. Both factors propagated the Mission with its inherent loftiness and splendour so that it won

partisans amongst the Medinan youth who promised the Messenger that they would propagate and protect the Mission until death. One of the consequences of this Emigration was that the fury and rancour of the polytheists increased as the opportunity to assassinate Muhammad escaped them, because they had gone to great efforts to attain it.

9. The period of enmity between the Moslems and the Jews in Medina. No sooner had the Messenger settled down there or it appeared that the Jews, whom he thought to be in favour of his Mission because they were People of the Book (*Ahl al-Kitāb*) and because they had previously asked his assistance in their wars against the Polytheists, denied his Mission and hatched plots against him and his companions. This induced him to extend his hand to them in order to prevent civil strife. He concluded a pact with them to the effect that he would leave them and their religion alone. By this treaty he felt to some extent safer. He then directed his concern and efforts to his original enemies who, after his Emigration, were pouring out their venom on his brothers who were prevented to emigrate because of their material circumstances, and who kept waiting for opportunities to oppose this mission and to scatter its adherents.

10. The period of provocation. The Prophet foresaw that unless he would take pains to propagate his Mission in Medina, which in fact was the task entrusted to him by his Lord, the Meccans would inevitably find a way to penetrate his new town and attack him by surprise, especially since the Jews with whom he had concluded a treaty were not so sincere that he could trust them to keep their pledge. It was not improbable that they would open up opportunities in Medina for the enemy outside and that they would subsequently join forces in order to expel the believers from Medina, as they had previously been expelled from Mecca.

For all these reasons the Messenger and his companions prepared themselves for resistance of those who opposed him and his Mission, the people of Mecca. He engaged in skirmishes with them and showed them his strength and his determination to continue with his Mission, to strive for its propagation and protection and to take pains to rescue "*the oppressed, men, women and children who say* : '*O our Lord, take us from this city of wrong-doing people* (*i.e. Mecca*), *and appoint for us from Thine own side a patron, and appoint for us from Thine side a helper*' " (K 4:75). This was the spirit wherein actual fighting between the believers and the polytheists began. Battles between both parties took place, some of which have been related in the Glorious Koran. Finally Allah crowned all these with the Conquest and Clear Victory.

11. The Jews break their pledge. The Jews had not been able to purify their hearts from the filth of rancour and envy. Allah's continuous favours to His Prophet and his faithful companions kindled the fire of antagonism in their hearts, which induced them to break the pledges they had concluded with the Messenger. This was done by Banū Qaynuqā', Banū al-Naḍīr and Banū Qurayẓah.[75] They all insulted the Messenger and defied the believers at a time when he had to keep the number of his adversaries as small as possible and to restrict the domain of fighting.

This is how Allah tried the faithful. They could not but denounce the pledge they had with them [i.e. the Jews] and enter a new stage in their relations, the stage of hostility and war after the stage and alliance.

These were the stages the Messenger went through, before and after the Emigration. It is obvious that the Polytheists of Mecca had been fighting the Prophet right from the start of his Mission, and that they were the first to commit aggression: time and again they chased the believers from their dwellings, they tyrannized the oppressed, subjecting them to all kinds of maltreatment and torture. It is also apparent that the Jews of Medina were only attacked by the Messenger after they had broken their pledge and had begun to offer resistance, just as the polytheists had done before.

From all these events it appears clearly that the Messenger only fought those who fought him, and that his fighting had no other aims than repelling oppression, warding off rebellion and aggression and putting an end to persecution for the sake of religion. And this is exactly what the verses regarding the reason for fighting prescribe, as we have seen before.

The wars that, after the death of the Messenger, were conducted by Abū Bakr and 'Umar were a completion of the building for which the Byzantines (*al-Rūm*) and the Persians (*al-Furs*) had laid the foundations with their own hands during the Prophet's lifetime. These two caliphs had no other choice than to repel evil, to give the people opportunities to hear the Message and to give security to the Moslems with regard to their religion and their countries.

On the strength of being a prophet, the Prophet sent his Mission to the kings of the Byzantines and the Persians. To the King of the Byzantines he dispatched his famous letter wherein he summoned him to be converted to Islam and held him, in case he refused, answerable for the sins of his people. When the letter had been translated for him, he assembled his patriarchs and high officials, submitted the letter to them and asked for their advice as to whether he should accept the summons or not. They then turned stubbornly away like donkeys and roared like lions, showing their disgust for his attitude with regard to the summons. However, he remained friendly with them, saying: "I have spoken these words to test your firmness concerning religion and kingship". Thus he abandoned his original intentions, preferring kingship over Islam. Then the officials and patriarchs began to sow the venomous seeds of hatred against the Mission and the Messenger in the hearts of commanders and subordinates. One of the consequences was that when Shuraḥbīl al-Ghassānī met the envoy of Allah's Messenger to the Prince of Buṣrā — at the time of the Mu'tah-affair [76] — and learnt what he came for and that he was an envoy of Mohammad, he gave orders to behead him. They surmised that the tolerance of the believers would not go so far as to condone such an attack on their honour. Therefore they intensified their alertness and assembled a force of Byzantines and Christian Arabs in order to liquidate Mohammed's case. When the Messenger heard this, he equipped an army to weaken the impetuosity of those who were aroused against him and mocked his Mission. As soon as this army reached the place were the envoy had been killed, they found the Byzantine troops in a state of alertness. The two armies clashed and fought fiercely. Three Moslem heroes were killed and had it not been for a stratagem that Allah disclosed to Khālid ibn al-Wālid, not a single soldier of the army would have escaped. After that there were continuous reports that the Byzantines were assembling troops against the Moslems, determined to attack them. Then the Prophet prepared himself and set out with an army before they could attack him in his own territory. When he arrived at Tabūk, he found out that they had abandoned their idea. The Prophet remained a few days, during which some princes concluded peace treaties with him. He then returned to Medina, thinking about those who missed the victory because of Khālid ibn al-Walīd's stratagem and assuming that they definitely would return. Therefore, he equipped an army under the command of Usāmah ibn Zayd. Immediately after this army had set out, Mohammed died. After this, Abū Bakr al-Ṣiddīq took over the command over the Moslems. He was of the opinion that firmness, loyalty and wisdom required that he dispatched the army the Messenger had prepared to counter the danger of these aggressors. After that, wars between the Moslems and the Byzantines followed in rapid succession until the Moslems conquered their lands and enabled the people to come to the Religion of Allah.

Just as thus the spirit of hostility of the Byzantines came to light, it manifested itself also among Persians. The Persians, however, were more arrogant and powerful than the Byzantines. All this became clear when the Messenger sent his letter to Kisrā.[77] The latter tore it to pieces and cast it on the floor out of haughtiness and arrogance. His presumption was to such an extent that he sent word to his governor in Yemen to send two strong men to Mohammed to take him with them. They actually came to the Messenger and informed him of the task they had to perform. Then the Messenger said: "This day Kisrā will be killed". Once the two men had learned that the words of the Messenger had come true, they became Moslems. Their conversion was the reason that the governor of Yemen was also converted. Afterwards al-Baḥrayn and 'Umān, countries that were also under Persian protection, were joined to Yemen. The Persians thought that the victory of the Moslems over the Byzantines was due only to the weakness of the Byzantine armies. They began to attack the neighbouring Arab tribes, employing thereby the kings of al-Ḥīrah, who applied themselves devotedly to aggression on the Moslems. Then the army of the Moslems set out against them and war broke out between them until the proxy of the Persian had to flee to al-Madā'in. So the kings of al-Ḥīrah surrendered to the Moslems. This fostered the hatred of the Persians against the Moslems. They became again conscious of their enormous power and equipped an army to expel the Moslems from their country. Fighting broke out and in the end the Moslems advanced to the lands of the Persians. So Kisrā's throne fell and all the Persians lands yielded to the helpers of Allah.

From this succinct exposé it will be clear that, in the first period, the Moslems only attacked people when they showed a spirit of hostility, opposition and resistance against the Mission and contempt for it. It also shows that when such a hostile spirit became manifest to them and they were convinced of its danger to themselves and to the Mission, they hastened to put it out of the way before its evil would grow beyond control. They did not wait for the enemy to attack them in their own country. This is in accordance with a natural sociological law: "Only contemptible people are fought in their own house". Nevertheless, one of their prescriptions was that, when they arrived in the land of an enemy whose hostility to them was evident, they let him choose one out of three things: conversion to Islam, poll-tax (*djizyah*) or fighting, in the hope that he would come to himself and that in his heart wisdom would get the upperhand over the spirit of enmity and antagonism. Read if you like some of the instructions of the Prophet to his army commanders: "*If you meet your heathen enemy, summon him to one of three things*",[78] then you will know that the [enemy's] spirit of hostility preceded the dispatchment of the [Moslem] army and that leaving the choice was only prompted by the hope for peace and abandonment of the spirit of hostility.

It also appears that the wars the Moslems conducted in the first period did not aim at forcing the people to the Religion, nor at subjugating or humiliating them, and that they were not prompted by greed for money or greater power.

In one's relations with the *dhimmī*'s, who are no adherents of Islam one should resort to the legislation of the Koran and also read how the Rightly Guided Caliphs [79] and the righteous army commanders dealt with those who were no adherents of Islam in order to know — on the basis of reason and evidence, not on the basis of supposition and conjecture — the extent of the tolerance of Islam in its treatment of its non-Moslem subjects and its love for universal peace and human solidarity. Then, one will also know how exalted its universal human laws are that attract people of their own free will and under the protection of which non-Moslems have lived continuously for centuries, without complaining about injustice and without offence to their rights.

I hope that after this exposé, the reader will not entertain doubts any longer as to the fact that the Koran and the Deeds of the Prophet together establish a theory concerning fighting, as I have described in this treatise. May Allah prepare us for the task, the Religion requires of us — of making known His laws and guidance, which guarantees the Moslems their power and honour. He is hearing and responsive.

NOTES

[1] Only the first chapter has been translated here.

[2] ʿAbdallāh Ibn al-Ḥasan (d. 145/762), a traditionist.

[3] As in most Islamic writings, the author assumes that the reader knows the Koran by heart, so that it was often sufficient to quote only a few words of the Koran texts. The reader was capable of completing them for himself. Here, the full text of each quotation will be given in the notes. Full text of K 2:216: "*Fighting is prescribed for you, though it is distasteful to you. Possibly ye may dislike a thing though it is good for you, and possibly ye may love a thing, though it is bad for you; Allah knoweth, though ye do not know*".

[4] Full text of K 9:122: "*It is not for the believers to march out all together, so why should not a party from each section of them march out, in order that they may gain understanding in religion, and that they may warn their people when they return to them, mayhap they will beware?*" For the original meaning of this verse, which almost certainly is not referring to going to war, cf. R. Paret. *Sure 9, 122 und der Ğihād. Welt des Islam*, n.s. II (1953),, pp. 232 ff.

[5] Full text of K 4:94: "*Those of the believers who sit still — other than those who have some injury — are not on a level with those who strive with goods and person in the way of Allah [i.e. those who take part in the jihad], and Allah hath bestowed upon those who serve, in preference to those who sit still, a mighty hire*".

[6] Full text of K 48:17: "*There is no blame upon the blind, or upon the lame, or upon the sick —; whosoever obeys Allah and His messenger He will cause him to enter Gardens through which the rivers flow; but whosoever turns away, He will inflict upon him a punishment painful*".

[7] Full text of K 9:91: "*No blame rests upon the frail or upon the sick or upon those who find nothing to contribute, if they are honest to Allah and His messenger; against those who do well there is no opening [lit. "way", i.e. to the infliction of punishment]; Allah is forgiving, compassionate*".

[8] The most important occurrence when the jihad becomes a personal obligation is an attack by the enemy on Islamic territory. All inhabitants of the area under attack — including women and slaves — are then obliged to expel the enemy.

[9] Djibrīl is the Arabic name for the archangel Gabriel. According to the Islamic doctrine, Allah's words were revealed to Mohammed through Djibrīl.

[10] Full text of K 8:39: "*Fight them until there is no dissension [i.e.*

persecution of the believers by the unbelievers] and the religion is entirely Allah's; if they desist, Allah of what they do is observant".

[11] Mālik Ibn Anas (d. 179/795), famous lawyer. The Traditions related by him were collected by his pupils in the compilation *al-Muwaṭṭa'*. The school founded on his doctrines, the Malikite, is still extant and counts its adherents chiefly in North Africa.

[12] This Tradition can be found in *al-Muwaṭṭa'* : jihad 10. However, Averroes' suggestion that we are dealing here with words of the Prophet must be a *lapsus*. The Tradition in question goes back to Abū Bakr. Cf. *al-Muwaṭṭa'* : jihad 10.

[13] Abū Bakr (d. 13/634), personal friend of Mohammed and after his death in the year 11/632, his successor (caliph). During his short reign, he subdued once more the revolting tribes of the Arabian Peninsula and made a beginning with the conquest of Syria and Iraq.

[14] Al-Ḥasan Ibn Muḥammad al-Tamīmī, a non-identified traditionist.

[15] Full text of K 47:4 : "*So when ye meet those who have disbelieved (let there be) slaughter until when ye have made havoc of them, bind (them) fast; then either freely or by ransom; until war lays down its burdens. That (is the rule); had Allah so willed, He would have vindicated himself upon them, but (this is) in order that He may try you one by the other; those who fight in the way of Allah — He will not send their works astray*".

[16] Full text of K 8:67 : "*It was not for a prophet to have prisoners so as to cause havoc in the land; ye intend the chance gains of this world but Allah intends the Hereafter; Allah is sublime, wise*". This verse is generally taken to have been a reproof at the address of Mohammed for his releasing on ransom most of the captives after the Battle of Badr. The phrase "*to cause havoc in the land*" goes to point out the danger that these released captives may, when occasion arises, attack the Moslems afresh.

[17] Abū 'Ubayd Sa'd Ibn 'Ubayd al-Zuhrī (d. 98/716), famous traditionist.

[18] 'Abd al-Mālik Ibn 'Abd al-'Azīz Ibn al-Mādjishūn (d. ca 213/827), Malikite lawyer.

[19] 'Abd al-Salām Ibn Sa'īd Ibn Ḥabīb al-Tanūkhī, known as Saḥnūn (d. 240/854), one of the best known early Malikite lawyers.

[20] Abū Ḥanīfah al-Nu'mān (d. 150/767), well-known lawyer. The School founded on his doctrines is called the Hanafite School and counts its adherents chiefly in the regions formerly belonging to the Ottoman empire and in Central Asia.

[21] He is only allowed to do this with the permission of his owner.

22 This remark is not entirely correct, cf. note 26. In view of its singular position in the context, it is possibly an interpolation.

23 For the full text of this Tradition, cf. p. 17.

24 Sufyān al-Thawrī (d. 161/778), famous traditionist and lawyer. A School founded on his doctrines existed for several centuries.

25 Al-Awzā'ī (d. 157/774), famous lawyer. Like the School of Thawrī, his School was superseded after a few centuries by other, still extant Schools.

26 Al-Shāfi'ī (d. 204/820), famous lawyer. He was the first to systematize the study of original sources (*'ilm al-uṣūl*) (cf. Introduction, p. 1-2). The Shafi'ite School derives its name from him and obtains its widest recognition along the borders of the Arabian Peninsula, in East Africa and in the Indian Archipelago. Occasionally, he is related to have given two different solutions for one and the same problem. Later generations of scholars decided which interpretation was the most authoritative.

27 For the full text of this Tradition, see p. 24.

28 Full text of K 9:5 : "*Then when the sacred months have slipped away, slay the polytheists wherever ye find them, seize them, beset them, lie in ambush for them everywhere*; *if they repent and establish the Prayer and pay the Zakāt, then set them free*; *Allah is forgiving compassionate*".

29 Dāwūd Ibn al-Haṣīn (d. 135/752-3), well-known traditionist.

30 'Ikrimah (d. 105/723-4), well-known traditionist. He was the slave of Ibn 'Abbās and many Traditions were related on his authority.

31 'Abdallāh Ibn al-'Abbās (d. 68/686-7). One of the Companions of the Prophet and one of the most important scholars among the first generation of Moslems.

32 Anas Ibn Mālik (d. ca. 92/710), well-known traditionist. In his youth, he was the Prophet's servant.

33 Abū Dāwūd (d. 275/888), author of one of the authoritative compilations of Traditions.

34 For the full text of K 9:5, see note 28.

35 During Mohammed's life, his relations with the unbelievers manifested a gradual escalation. This escalation is reflected in the Koran. In his Meccan period, he attempted to win the unbelievers by persuasion and arguments. When this failed, it was revealed that the believers should leave the unbelievers alone. The verse determining that polytheists may only be fought if they make the first move (K 2:190) dates from the beginning of his Medinese period. At last the verses were revealed which gave the absolute command to fight the unbelievers (K 2:216, K 9:5 — the verse of the Sword —

and K 9:29). According to most scholars, this command cancelled all previous verses with regard to the relations with unbelievers.

36 Sumrah Ibn Djundub al-Fazāri (d. 59/678-9), well-known traditionist.

37 Zayd Ibn Wahb (d. 96/714-5), well known traditionist.

38 ʿUmar Ibn al-Khaṭṭāb (d. 23/644), second caliph of the Islam and successor of Abū Bakr (see note 18). During his reign, which lasted for ten years (13/634-23/644), Syria, Iraq and Egypt were conquered. He is regarded as the founder of the organization of the Islamic state.

39 This Tradition has not been included in any of the authoritative compilations.

40 For the full text, see note 28.

41 Al-Layth Ibn Saʿd (d. 175/791-2), well-known lawyer and traditionist.

42 Full text of K 48:25 : "*They are the ones who have disbelieved, and have turned aside from the sacred mosque, both you and the offering prevented from reaching its place (of sacrifice). Had it not been for men and women who were believers, whom ye did not know, lest ye should have trampled them and disgrace fallen upon you unwittingly on their account — in order that Allah may cause to enter into His mercy whomsoever He willeth — had they been separated out, We should have inflicted upon those of them who have disbelieved a punishment painful*".

43 Full text of K 17:15 : "*Whosoever lets himself be guided does so to his own benefit, and whosoever goes astray, does so to his own hurt; no burden-bearer bears the burden of another; We have not been accustomed to punish until We have sent a messenger*".

44 After the Emigration (*Hidjrah*) in the year 622 it became obligatory for fresh converts to Islam to emigrate to Medina and to join the other Moslems. After the conquest of Mecca in 8/630 this obligation fell into abeyance according to most scholars.

45 Sometimes there is controversy about the qualification of a certain act. It may, for instance, be obligatory according to some, and a matter of indifference according to others. In order to reconcile these opinions, it is often assumed that the act in question is recommendable.

46 Full text of K 8:66 : "*Now Allah hath made it lighter for you and knoweth that there is weakness among you; so 'If there be a hundred of you who endure, they will overcome two hundred, and if there be a thousand of you, they will overcome two thousand, by the permission of Allah; Allah is with those who endure'* ". This verse has abrogated the previous one, K 8:65 : "*O thou prophet, stir up the believers to fight : 'If there be twenty of you who*

endure, they will overcome two hundred, and if there be a hundred of you, they will overcome a thousand of those who have disbelieved, because they are a people of no intelligence' ".

47 In the year 6/628, Mohammed concluded a peace treaty with the Meccans for a period of ten years. However, when the Meccans began to incite to rebellion some troops that were allied to Mohammed, he broke off the treaty and attacked Mecca, which he conquered in the year 8/639.

48 For the full text, see note 28.

49 Full text of K 9:29 : "*Fight against those who do not believe in Allah nor in the Last Day, and do not make forbidden what Allah and His Messenger have made forbidden, and do not practice the religion of truth, of those who have been given the Book, until they pay the jizya (i.e. poll-tax, djizyah) off-hand, being subdued*".

50 Full text of K 8:61 : "*If they incline to make peace, incline thou to it, and set thy trust upon Allah; verily He is the Hearer, the Knower*".

51 In the year 5/627, the Meccans besieged Medina with the assistance of some Bedouin tribes, the Confederates. These tribes had come along with the Meccans in prospect of financial reward. Mohammed attempted to bribe one of these tribes into moving away. At first, this tribe, Ghaṭafān, demanded half of the Medinese date-harvest, but when after some negotiating they had agreed on a third, the citizens of Medina remonstrated. However, before matters had been settled, Mohammed had succeeded in expelling the Meccans and their allied tribes in the Battle of the Ditch.

52 Abū Thawr (d. 240/854), well-known lawyer. A school founded on his doctrines existed for a few centuries only.

53 Full text of K 8:40 : "*Fight them until there is no dissension and the religion is entirely Allah's; if they desist, Allah of what they do is observant*".

54 See p. 20.

55 The ninth chapter of the Koran, called *Sūrat Barā'ah* or *Sūrat al-Tawbah*, is considered as the last chapter revealed.

56 In the year 8/630.

57 For the full text, see note 44.

58 For the full text, see note 49.

59 In K 7:157-8, Mohammed is called "*al-nabī al-ummī*". According to traditional Islamic Koran interpretation these words mean : "the illiterate prophet". Mohammed being illiterate enhances the miracle of the Koran. Modern research, however, has demonstrated that in this verse the word *ummī* means "non-Jewish" or "heathen".

[60] The *textus receptus* of this verse reads "*to those who are being fought*" (*li-alladhīn yuqātalūn*). A critical examination of the historical facts supports the alternative reading: "*to those who are fighting*" (*li-alladhīn yuqātilūn*). According to the first reading permission is granted to fight back against attacks from the enemy, whereas, according to the latter reading, permission to fight is granted to those who were already fighting against oppression.

[61] In the Koran, the words: "*in the way of Allah*" (*fī sabīl Allāh*) are often added to the word for fighting in order to emphasize its religious sanction and to distinguish it from other forms of fighting that are not allowed.

[62] Abū Yūsuf Ya'qūb (d. 182/798), a well known lawyer and pupil of Abū Ḥanīfah.

[63] Abū 'Ubaydah (d. 18/639), army commander during the reign of 'Umar.

[64] For the full text of this Tradition, see p. 24.

[65] This is the opinion of the Hanafite School. For the opinions of the other Schools, consult pp. 23-25.

[66] Fakhr al-Dīn Abū 'Abd Allāh Muḥammad al-Rāzī (d. 606/1209), famous theologian and philosopher.

[67] Abū al-Thanā' Maḥmūd Shihāb al-Dīn al-Ālūsī (d. 1270/1854), Islamic scholar and author of a Koran commentary.

[68] After Mohammed's death in 632, many tribes of the Arabian Peninsula revolted. During the reign of Abū Bakr (632-4) they were again subdued by Abū Bakr's army commander Khālid ibn al-Walīd. In one of the battles, the Battle of Yamāmah, the Moslems suffered heavy losses. According to the traditional story, there were many Koran reciters among those who were killed. As the Koran, at that time, had not yet been put down in writing, this incidence induced Abū Bakr to give orders to compile the Koran in writing. Contemporary research has shown that this story is probably a later invention.

[69] The Tabūk campaign took place in the year 9/630.

[70] Full text of K 33:12-20: "*The Hypocrites and those in whose hearts is disease were saying: 'Allah and His messenger have promised us nothing but illusion'. A party of them said: 'O my people of Yathrib, there is no abiding place for you, so return'; and a part of them were asking leave of the prophet, saying: 'Our houses are a weak point'; they were not a weak point, they were only wishing to flee. If an entrance had been made upon them from that side (on the side on which their houses stood) and they had been asked (to join in)*

sedition, they would have joined in it and would have hesitated with it but slightly. Yet they had covenanted with Allah previously that they would not turn their backs; the covenant of Allah is (a thing the fulfilment of which is) to be required. Say: 'Flight will not benefit you, if ye flee from death or from being killed; in that case ye will not enjoy life, except for a little'. Say: 'Who is there that will defend you from Allah, if He intends evil against you, or intends mercy towards you?' They will not find for themselves apart from Allah, either patron or helper. Allah knows fairly well those among you who hinder, and who say to their brethren: 'Come hither to us' and who come not to attack except seldom, being niggardly towards you. When fear comes, one sees them looking at one, with their eyes rolling like one who faints at the point of death; but when fear passes away, they scarify you with sharp tongues, niggardly of good things. These have not believed, and Allah hath made their works of no avail; for Allah that is easy. They think that the Confederates have not gone away; if the Confederates come, they will wish that they were living in the desert among the Bedouin, inquiring for news of you, and if they should be amongst you, they would not fight except a little."

71 For the original meaning of this verse, see note 4.

72 One of the clans of the Quraysh tribe. Mohammed's family belonged to this clan.

73 Mohammed's uncle, who took care of him after his father and grandfather had died.

74 The tribe that inhabited the town of al-Ṭā'if, situated ca. 45 miles S.E. of Mecca.

75 The names of the Jewish tribes in Medinah.

76 With the Mu'tah-affair the author refers to the military expedition sent by Mohammed in the year 8/629 in order to punish Shuraḥbīl.

77 Kisrā is the Arabic name of the Persian emperor Chosroes.

78 For the full text of this Tradition, see p. 20.

79 The first four successors of Mohammed are usually called the "Rightly Guided Caliphs".

BIBLIOGRAPHY

1. GENERAL WORKS ON JIHAD

Muhammad Hamidullah, *Muslim Conduct of State.* [3] Lahore : Sh. Muhammad Ashraf, 1953. 389 p.

Majid Khadduri, *War and Peace in the Law of Islam.* Baltimore : The Johns Hopkins Press, 1955, 321 p.

Albrecht Noth, *Heiliger Krieg und Heiliger Kampf in Islam und Christentum. Beiträge zur Vorgeschichte und Geschichte der Kreuzzüge.* Bonn : Ludwig Röhrscheid Verl., 1966. 160 p. Bonner Historische Forschungen, 28.

Rudolph Peters, *Djihād : War of aggression or defense?* In : *Akten des VII. Kongresses für Arabistik und Islamwissenschaft.* (Göttingen, 15-22. August 1974). Göttingen, 1976. P. 282-290.

F. Schwally, *Der heilige Krieg des Islam in Religionsgeschichtlicher und staatsrechtlicher Bedeutung.* In : *Intern. Monatsschr. f. Wissensch. Kunst u. Technik,* 1916, p. 678-714.

2. TRANSLATIONS OF CLASSICAL SOURCES ON JIHAD

a. *Hanafite School*

Abū Yusūf (d. 182/798), *Kitāb al-Kharādj.*

E. Fagnan, *Le livre de l'impôt foncier.* Paris : Paul Geuthner, 1921, p. 27-36, 290-320.

Muḥammad Ibn al-Ḥasan al-Shaybānī (d. 189/804), *Kitāb al-Siyar.*

Majid Khadduri, *The Islamic Law of Nations. Shaybani's Siyar.* Baltimore : The Johns Hopkins Press, 1966. 311 p.

Aḥmad al-Qudūri (d. 428/1037), *al-Mukhtaṣar.*

L. Bercher, *Le Livre de la guerre sainte. Revue Tunisienne de Droit,* 2 (1954), p. 123-49.

Ch. Solvet, *Institut du droit mahométan sur la guerre avec les infidèles.* Paris : 1829.

Burhān al-Dīn Maḥmud al-Maḥbūbī (d. 7th/13th century), *Wiqāyat al-Riwāyah.*

B. Haneberg, *Das Muslimische Kriegsrecht.* Abh. d. bayer. Ak. d. Wissensch., Philos.-Philol. Cl. 12 Bd, 2. Abth. München : 1870. p. 276-290.

Muḥammad Ibn ʿAlī al-Ḥaṣkafī (d. 1088/1677), *al-Durr al-Mukhtār sharḥ Tanwīr al-Abṣār.*

Brij Mohan Dayal, *The Durr al-Mukhtār, being the well-known commentary of the Tanwīr al-Absār of Muḥammad ibn ʿAbdallah al-Tamartashi.* Lucknow : 1913.

b. *Malikite School*

Ibn Abī Zayd al-Qayrawānī (d. 386/996), *al-Risālah.*

L. Bercher, *La risāla ou Epître sur les éléments du dogme et la loi de l'Islam selon le rite Mālikite.* Algiers : Jules Carbonel, 1949, p. 162-7, 291.

E. Fagnan, *Risala ou traité abrégé de droit malékite et morale musulmane.* Paris : Paul Geuthner, 1914. p. 107-10, 231.

ʿAlī Ibn ʿAbd al-Raḥmān Ibn Hudhayl al-Andalusī (d. end of the 8th/14th century). *Tuḥfat al-anfus wa-shiʿār sukkān al-Andalus.*

Louis Mercier, *L'Ornement des âmes et la devise des habitants d'el Andalus. Traité de Guerre Sainte Islamique.* Paris : Paul Geuthner, 1939. 349 p.

Khalīl Ibn Isḥāq (d. 767/1365), *al-Mukhtaṣar.*

J. Guidi and D. Santillana, *Il Muḫtaṣar, sommario del diritto malechita di Ḫalil.* 2 vols. Milan : Ulrico Hoepli, 1919. Vol. 1, p. 385-424.

E. Fagnan, *Le Djihad ou guerre sainte.* Algiers : 1908.

A. Perron, *Précis de jurisprudence musulmane.* Exploration scientifique de l'Algérie pendant les années 1840-42. Paris : 1844-54, vols. 10-15.

c. *Shafiʿite School*

ʿAlī Ibn Muḥammad al-Māwardī (d. 450/1058). *Kitāb al-Aḥkām al-Sulṭāniyyah.*

E. Fagnan, *Les statuts governementaux ou règles du droit public et administratif.* Algiers : Adolphe Jourdan, 1915. p. 71-131, 267-99.

Abū Isḥāq Ibrāhīm al-Shirāzī (d. 476/1083), *Kitāb al-Tanbīh.*

G. H. Bousquet, *Kitāb at-Tanbīh ou le Livre de l'Admonition.* 4 vols. Algiers : La Maison des Livres, 1949-52. Vol. 4, p. 35-51.

Abū Shudjāʿ (d. 593/1196), *al-Taqrīb fī al-Fiqh.*

S. Keyzer, *Précis de jurisprudence musulmane selon le rite Chaféite.* Leyden : E. J. Brill, 1859. P. 52-4.

G. H. Bousquet, *Abrégé de la loi musulmane selon le rite de l'Imam El-Chafi. Revue Algérienne,* 1935. I, p. 193-207; 1936, I, 1-16, 48-52, 66-72, 78-86.

Abū Zakarīyā Yaḥyā al-Nawawī (d. 676/1278), *Minhādj al-Ṭālibīn.*

L. W. C. van den Berg, *Le Guide des Zélés Croyants. Manuel de jurisprudence selon le rite de Chāfi'i.* 3 vols. Batavia : Imprimerie du Gouvernement, 1882-4. Vol. 3, p. 255-88 (see, however, the corrections in Bousquet's translation of Shīrāzī).

Badr al-Dīn Ibn Djāmā'ah (d. 733/1333), *Taḥrīr al-Aḥkām fī Tadbīr Millat al-Islām.*

Hans Kofler, *Ibn Ǧamā'a's Handbuch des islamischen Staats- und Verwaltungsrecht. Islamica* VII (1935), p. 35-64, Schlussheft (1938), p. 18-130.

Ibn Qāsim al-Ghazzī (d. 918/1522), *Fatḥ al-Qarīb* (cmt. on *al-Taqrīb fī al-Fiqh* by Abū Shudjā').

L. W. C. van den Berg, *La Révélation de l'Omniprésent.* Leyden : E. J. Brill, 1894. P. 604-31 (see, however, the corrections in Bousquet's transl. of Shīrāzī).

d. *Hanbalite School*

'Abdallāh Ibn Aḥmad Ibn Qudāmah (d. 620/1223), *al-'Umdah fī Aḥkām al-Fiqh.*

H. Laoust, *Le précis de droit d'Ibn Qudāma.* Beirut : Institut Français de Damas, 1950. P. 271-81..

Taqī al-Dīn Ibn Taymiyyah (d. 728/1238), *al-Siyāsah al-Shar'iyyah.*

H. Laoust, *Le traité de droit public d'Ibn Taimiyah. Tr. ann. de la Siyāsah Šar'iyyah.* Beirut : Institut Français de Damas, 1948. P. 122-36.

Omar A. Farrukh, *On public and Private Law in Islam, or Public Policy in Islamic Jurisprudence.* Beirut : Khayat's, 1966. P. 135-63.

e. *Shi'ite works*

Al-Muḥaqqiq al-Ḥillī (d. 676/1277), *Sharā'i' al-Islām fī Masā'il al-Ḥalāl wa-al-Ḥarām.*

A. Querry, *Droit Musulman. Recueil de lois concernant les Musulmans schyites.* 2 vols. Paris : Imprimerie Nationale, 1871-2. Vol. 1, p. 321-5.

3. RECENT ISLAMIC WRITINGS ON JIHAD IN WESTERN LANGUAGES

Khalifa Abd al-Hakim, *War and Peace.* In : Aziz Ahmad en G. E. von Grunebaum, *Muslim Self-statement in India and Pakistan, 1858-1968.* Wiesbaden : Harrassowitz, 1970. P. 182-9.

Muhammad Abu Zahra, *Begriff des Krieges im Islam.* Aus dem Ar. übers. v. Prof. Dr. Omar Amin von Leers, revidiert v. Dr. Ezz El-Din Ismail. Cairo : Der Oberste Rat für Islamische Angelegenheiten, n.d. 73 p.

Mohamed Abu Zahra, *International Relations in Islam.* In : *The first Conference of the Academy of Islamic Research.* Cairo : S.O.P.-Press, 1383/1964, p. 187-236.

Mawlawi Cheragh Ali, *A Critical Exposition of Popular Jihad* : Calcutta : Thecker, Spink & Co., 1885, civ+227+249 p.

Najib Armanazi, *L'Islam et le droit international.* Thèse. Paris : 1929. 162 p.

Mohamed Aly Bechebichy, *Les relations internationales islamiques.* Tr. p. Ibrahim el-Mouwelhy, rev. p. Ahmed Rachad. Cairo : Conseil Supérieur des Affairs Islamiques, 1966. 56 p.

Mohammed Talaat al-Ghunaimi, *The Muslim Conception of International Law and the Western Approach.* The Hague : Martinus Nijhoff, 1968. 228 p.

Abu Said Mohammad Husain, *A Treatise on jihad.* Tr. fr. Urdu. 2nd impr. Lahore : Victoria Press, 1887, 32 p.

J. Jomier, *Le Commentaire Coranique du Manar.* Paris : Maisonneuve, 1954. P. 251-81 (summarizes the ideas of Muḥammad ʿAbduh and Muḥammad Rashīd Riḍā).

Zafrullah Khan, *Islam and International Relations. Internationale Spectator* (The Hague) 10 (1956), nr. 11, p. 308-22.

Ahmed Rechid, *l'Islam et le droit des gens.* In : *Recueil des Cours. Académie de droit international,* 1937 (Paris : 1938). Vol. II, p. 375-504.

Aslam Siddiqi, *Djihad, an Instrument of Islamic Revolution. Islamic Studies* 2 (1963), p. 383-98.